D1168325

Ron Howard
Child Star & Hollywood Director

Barbara Kramer

Enslow Publishers, Inc.

44 Fadem Road	PO Box 38
Box 699	Aldershot
Springfield, NJ 07081	Hants GU12 6BP
USA	UK

Library of Congress Cataloging-in-Publication Data

Kramer, Barbara.
    Ron Howard : child star & Hollywood director / Barbara Kramer.
        p.   cm. — (People to know)
    Includes bibliographical references and index.
    Summary: Presents the life and career of Ron Howard who gained
fame as a young actor starring in television shows and went on to
become a film director and producer.
    ISBN 0-89490-981-9
    1. Howard, Ron—Juvenile literature. 2. Motion picture producers
and directors—United States—Biography—Juvenile literature.
3. Actors—United States—Biography—Juvenile literature.
[1. Howard, Ron. 2. Motion picture producers and directors.
3. Actors and actresses.] I. Title. II. Series.
PN1998.3.H689K73 1998
791.43'0233'092—dc21
[B]   97-43577
                                             CIP
                                           AC

Printed in the United States of America

10 9 8 7 6 5 4 3 2 1

Illustration Credits: Archive Photos, pp. 15, 17, 19, 21, 32, 34; Buena
Vista/Archive Photos, p. 52; Darlene Hammond/Archive Newsphotos, pp. 4,
66; Fotos International/Archive Photos, p. 93; Frank Edwards/Fotos
International/Archive Photos, p. 36; Keith Hamshere/Lucasfilm/Archive
Photos, p. 72; Lorey Sebastian/Touchstone Pictures/Archive Photos, p. 97;
New World Pictures/Archive Photos, p. 42; Phillip Caruso/Fotos
International/Archive Photos, p. 79; Ron Batzdorff/Archive Photos, p. 8;
Santiago Rodriquez/Archive Photos, p. 26; 20th Century Fox/Archive Photos,
pp. 58, 60; Victor Malafronte/Archive Newsphotos, p. 85.

Cover Illustration: Victor Malafronte/Archive Newsphotos

Contents

Ron Howard

Filming in the Vomit Comet

It was March 25, 1996—the day of the sixty-eighth annual Academy Awards presentations. By 4:00 P.M., limousines were already arriving at the Dorothy Chandler Pavilion in Los Angeles, California, the site of the film industry's yearly ceremony. Excited movie fans gathered near the entrance of the pavilion, hoping to catch a glimpse of their favorite Hollywood personalities. They cheered as men in tuxes and women in designer gowns stepped out of vehicles and strolled across the red carpet leading up to the building's entrance.

A familiar face among the celebrities was director Ron Howard. His black tuxedo was quite a change for him. Usually, he wore casual clothes—tennis shoes, blue jeans or baggy pants, and a baseball cap. "I didn't even own a tuxedo until 1991," he once said. "I was strictly a rental man."[1]

The top of his head was almost bald now. Otherwise, he still looked very much like the redheaded, freckle-faced boy who once played Opie Taylor on the popular television series *The Andy Griffith Show*.

The Academy Award nominees had been announced in February. Howard's latest film, *Apollo 13*, received nine nominations, including Best Picture. However, much of the talk during the past month had been about the nomination the film did *not* get—Best Director.

Nine out of ten times that honor went to the winner of the Directors Guild of America (DGA) prize, which is awarded a few weeks before the Academy Awards. Howard was chosen Best Director by the DGA, but the Academy Awards committee snubbed him.

When the Academy Awards nominations were announced, Howard appeared to be amused by that snub. "There will be a little controversy that I got the DGA and not an Academy nomination," he said, "and I'll enjoy that."[2]

The movie *Apollo 13* tells the true story of the third planned landing on the moon. That space flight was launched on April 11, 1970, with three astronauts on board—Jim Lovell, Fred Haise, and Jack Swigert. Two days later, an oxygen tank exploded in the command module, the main part of the *Apollo* spacecraft. As oxygen seeped out of the command module, the astronauts crowded into the lunar module.

The lunar module was the small vehicle used to land on the moon. It was meant to keep two astronauts alive for two days. Now it would have to keep three astronauts alive for almost four days. They were about two hundred thousand miles from earth, and it would take those four days to bring them home.

How would the astronauts survive? That was the question on everyone's mind at Mission Control in Houston, Texas.

Mission Control is a room filled with computers that monitor every part of a space mission. The people who work there are experts in space flight and the spacecraft used in those missions. For the next few days, they worked around the clock trying to find a way to bring the astronauts home. Finally, after four tension-filled days, the astronauts splashed down safely.

Howard had the difficult job of making the *Apollo 13* movie suspenseful even though everyone already knew the ending. He did it by paying careful attention to detail.

One of the challenges he faced was recreating an exact replica of the *Apollo* spacecraft. Astronaut David Scott was hired as a technical advisor for the film. He said that the remaking of that spacecraft was very accurate. "There must be more than 400 controls, switches, circuit breakers, buttons and lights in the spacecraft," Scott noted. "I spent about three months looking at them all and found just one little, insignificant thing wrong: the color of a small scribe on a window."[3]

During the real *Apollo 13* flight, the astronauts

Ron Howard at work on the set of Apollo 13.

had to shut down everything on the spacecraft to save energy. They knew they would need that power later to reenter the earth's atmosphere at the end of the flight. Without power, temperatures quickly dropped until it was so cold inside the lunar module that the astronauts could see their breath.

Tom Hanks was hired to play the role of Jim Lovell, commander of the *Apollo 13* mission. Bill Paxton and Kevin Bacon starred as the other two astronauts on the flight. As actors, they could pretend to be cold, but the only way to make their breath visible was to lower the temperature on the set.

Howard brought in huge refrigeration units to keep the set at a cold thirty-four degrees Fahrenheit during the last five weeks of filming. That is only two degrees above freezing, but Howard got no complaints from the actors. "They knew what they were getting themselves into," he noted, "and everyone on this movie was dedicated to telling the story."[4]

The most amazing scenes in the movie are those in which the astronauts float in the weightlessness of space. For the first time ever in a movie, the filming was done in actual weightless conditions. The National Aeronautics and Space Administration (NASA) gave Howard its full support in filming the movie. He was allowed to use NASA's KC-135 training jet to film the weightlessness scenes.

The jet, nicknamed the Vomit Comet, has a completely stripped down cargo area with padded walls. The pilot flies large arcs, called parabolas. For each parabola, the jet soars to an altitude of thirty-six thousand feet, then makes a sharp dive. For about thirty seconds, when the jet is at the top of the arc, the passengers are weightless.

Before filming began, Howard and the actors flew in the Vomit Comet just to get the feel of weightlessness. "We were all scared to death," Howard recalled.[5] They had been warned that the flight might make them sick. This worried Howard, who often suffered from motion sickness. "As the director, I kept thinking, all right now, if I'm the first one to hurl are they going to like all lose respect for me or what?" he said.[6] Luckily, he did not get sick.

After a few flights to get used to being weightless, they began to practice moving from one point to another. The final stage was to bring in the command module and the lunar module and bolt them to the floor of the KC-135. Then filming began. In zero gravity, or weightlessness, there is no up or down. "So I was upside down with my little megaphone shouting out directions," Howard explained.[7]

Howard got four hours of weightlessness on film, captured in blocks of about thirty seconds each. That was the amount of time the actors were weightless on each parabola. "The actors playing astronauts actually spent more time in the zero-gravity plane than any real astronaut ever did," Lovell noted.[8]

The result is an exciting movie. In a review for *Entertainment Weekly*, Owen Gleiberman wrote: "Visually, the film's re-creation of space travel is flat-out stunning."[9] In a review for *People*, Ralph Novak called the film "a combined barn burner, flag-waver, tearjerker and edge-of-the-seater."[10]

At the 1996 Academy Awards ceremonies, *Apollo 13*

won in two categories—film editing and sound. The actor/director Mel Gibson won the award for Best Director for his movie *Braveheart*. Ironically, at that time Howard was directing Gibson in the movie *Ransom*.

The two friends joked about the fact that Howard was now directing the Best Director, but there were no hurt feelings. Howard had been in the entertainment business too long to get upset about awards. He was only forty-two years old, but he already had forty years of experience in show business.

Ron Howard grew up in front of television audiences. For eight years he played Opie Taylor in *The Andy Griffith Show*. Later, he starred as Richie Cunningham in *Happy Days*. In spite of his success in front of the camera, Howard's real dream was to work behind the camera as a director.

2

Opie

Ron Howard got his start in show business long before *The Andy Griffith Show* debuted in 1960. His first acting job was in a play that his dad directed, *The Seven Year Itch*. He was only a year and a half old then, and everyone called him Ronny.

Ronald William Howard was born on March 1, 1954, in Duncan, Oklahoma, but he spent most of his early years in New York City. His dad, Rance Howard, was an actor and director. Ronny's mother, Jean, was an actress, but after Ronny was born she spent most of her time as an at-home mom.

One summer Rance Howard was directing a play called *Mr. Roberts*. Jean Howard was in the play, and

Ronny hung out at the theater, watching them work. For fun, he began to repeat the lines of Ensign Pulver, one of the characters. "We developed this game where my dad played Mr. Roberts and I played Pulver," Howard recalled.[1] After that, they began doing other scenes and Rance Howard decided that maybe his son could do some acting.

When Ronny was two years old, he appeared in the television show *Police Station*. He made his film debut when he was four. Later, Rance Howard told a reporter how his son got that part. "I was seeing a casting director in New York about a job," Rance Howard explained. "He happened to be looking for a child for a film called *The Journey*. I told him I had a son. The next day I brought Ronny in, and that was that."[2]

Ronny and his parents flew to Vienna, Austria, where *The Journey* was being shot on location. When they returned to the United States, they moved to California. They settled in Burbank, where Ronny's brother, Clint, was born on April 20, 1959.

The move was a big boost for Ronny's acting career. Directors were impressed with his ability to memorize lines. He made guest appearances on several television series, including *Dennis the Menace*, *The Many Loves of Dobie Gillis*, and *The Twilight Zone*. Then came *The Andy Griffith Show*, which debuted on October 3, 1960.

That series—still shown on cable television—is about the everyday events in the lives of the people in the fictional town of Mayberry. Andy Griffith stars as Sheriff Andy Taylor, and Ronny is his son, Opie.

Another regular on the show is Frances Bavier in the role of Aunt Bee. She lives with the Taylors and helps take care of Opie. Comedian Don Knotts plays Barney Fife, Sheriff Taylor's deputy.

Although he got an early start, Howard said he never felt he was pushed into acting. "It was something I did with my dad, so when I started doing it with other people it was just a matter of playing the game with them, something I did for fun," he recalled.[3] His parents always said that he could quit at any time if he did not enjoy it.

On the other hand, Rance Howard told Ronny that if he was going to act, he had to be professional. One time during the first year of *The Andy Griffith Show*, Ronny misbehaved on the set and his father picked him up and spanked him. "He explained that I had to be responsible, that people were trying to work," Howard said.[4]

Rance Howard also looked out for his son. He asked the adults not to tease Ronny or horse around with him on the set. He said that it was hard for a child to know when it was time to joke around and when it was time to get down to work. It would be easier for Ronny if they did not confuse him.

Rance Howard was always on the set helping his son with his lines. On Thursdays, the cast, writers, and the director would get together for script readings. Since Ronny could not yet read when he first started the show, his father read Opie's part.

Everyone could give an opinion about a script at those meetings, even Ronny. The first time Ronny spoke up was when they were reading the script for

Ronny Howard was only six years old when he began playing Opie Taylor, the son of Sheriff Taylor, on The Andy Griffith Show.

the second episode of the second season. He recalled how excited he got when the rest of the cast took his suggestion seriously. He had a big grin on his face, and someone asked him why he was smiling. "I told them that that was the first time anyone had ever taken my advice," Howard said.[5]

Ronny's parents wanted him to have a normal life away from the set. Being mobbed by adoring fans was not normal for a child. To avoid that, Ronny's parents had a special clause written into his contract. It said that he did not have to make publicity tours to promote the show.

When Ronny was working, he was tutored on the set. In the spring, when filming ended for the year, he went to a public school. At first, his classmates were impressed by the fact that he was a child star, but Howard remembers that the attention died down quickly.

Howard also remembers being the target of jokes because of his television role. It was unfortunate for him that his character's name, Opie, rhymed with dopey. As he got older, kids sometimes called him Opium. "I'd have to get into fights with people," Howard said. "Fortunately, I could sort of hang in."[6]

Jean Howard and Ronny's brother, Clint, were frequent visitors on the set of *The Andy Griffith Show*. The family ate lunch together, or sometimes Jean and Clint just stayed at the studio so that the family could have time together.

During the third season, Clint made the first of four guest appearances on the show. He played Leon, the silent boy who was always dressed in a cowboy

Ronny Howard with other cast members from The Andy Griffith Show. *Pictured, left to right, are Aneta Corsaut, who played Opie Taylor's teacher, Helen Crump; Frances Bavier as Aunt Bee; and Andy Griffith as Sheriff Andy Taylor.*

outfit. Clint later went on to star in his own series, *Gentle Ben*. His co-star, Gentle Ben, was a bear.

Ronny was always interested in what other people did on the show. He became friends with the cameramen, who let him look through the camera, adjust the lenses, and push the dollies around. By the time Ronny was eight years old, he had discovered that "the directors were the ones who made things happen."[7]

The director is the one who controls all the different parts of a television or movie production, including set design, costuming, and filming. The director hires the actors and tells them what to do. It is also the director's job to complete filming on time and stay within the budget. Ronny knew, even as a child, that he wanted to be a director some day.

He began doing some filming of his own. "The producer of the show gave me an eight-millimeter camera and my dad and I would shoot little movies I made up," Howard said.[8]

In addition to *The Andy Griffith Show*, Ronny had several movie roles. He had a part in a film called *Five Minutes to Live*, which was released in 1961. (It was re-released in 1966 as *Door-to-Door Maniac*.)

He learned to talk with a lisp for his part in the film version of *The Music Man* (1962). He plays Winthrop, the younger brother of Marian the Librarian. He even sang for that role. A reviewer of the movie described Ronny as "a pint-sized kid whose talents know no dimension."[9]

In 1963, Ronny starred as Eddie in the film *The Courtship of Eddie's Father*. Two years later he appeared in another movie, *Village of the Giants*.

Shirley Jones and Ronny Howard in The Music Man. *Ronny had to learn to talk with a lisp for his role as Winthrop, the younger brother of Marian the Librarian, played by Jones.*

Although he was busy with acting, Ronny also found time for his favorite sport—baseball. "As a kid he never missed one Little League game," Griffith noted. "We shot around him."[10]

One of Ronny's favorite episodes of *The Andy Griffith Show* was titled "The Ball Game." One reason he liked it so much was that it was about baseball. Another reason he liked it was that his dad had written the script and it was based on a true story.

Ronny's parents had taken him and some of his friends to a park to play softball. Rance Howard was the umpire. During the game, he called Ronny out on a play at the plate. Ronny thought he was safe and so did some of his friends. The call set off an argument involving Ronny, his friends, and his family. Rance Howard thought it would make a good episode for *The Andy Griffith Show*. He went to work on the script. In that episode, Sheriff Taylor is the umpire who calls his son out at the plate.

People wondered if Ronny Howard was really like the character he played. "I think that the two were very close," Howard later said. "Oh, there were some things that the writers would have Opie doing that I would have never done, of course. But I think—particularly as the show developed—that they wrote with my own personality in mind."[11]

Andy Griffith admitted that the relationship between Sheriff Taylor and Opie was actually based on Ronny's relationship with his real dad. However, Ronny and Griffith were also close. "Andy was like a wonderful uncle to me," Howard recalled.[12]

Howard says he learned a lot about comedy from

Nine-year-old Ronny with his four-year-old brother, Clint, on the set of The Andy Griffith Show. *Clint Howard made guest appearances as Leon, the silent boy who was always dressed as a cowboy.*

Griffith. "I best remember him sitting around the reading table telling us that it was important for the show to be funny, but it had to be funny because the viewer could identify with the characters and not because we were a bunch of hayseeds and dumb hicks," Howard explained.[13]

The easygoing Griffith liked a calm set. "The atmosphere was real relaxed and very professional," Howard said. "And it was fun. A lot of laughter."[14]

Ronny enjoyed his time on the set so much that he hated to see the season end. "I used to cry every year when the show went on hiatus," he said.[15]

It was a contrast to some of his other acting experiences. He remembered one time when he was not able to cry for a movie scene. The director threatened to beat him so that he would cry. Ronny did not think that would happen. "My dad was there and I figured my dad would punch him out if he tried something," Howard later explained.[16]

The Andy Griffith Show lasted eight seasons, and it was always rated in the Top 10. Television history includes a long list of children who star in a series and then are never heard from again when the show goes off the air. Fourteen-year-old Ronny Howard was not one of them.

American Graffiti

T*he Andy Griffith Show* ended its eight-year run in 1968, but Ronny kept on working. He made guest-starring appearances in several television series, including *Judd for the Defense*, *Gunsmoke*, and *The FBI*.

When he was not working, Ronny attended Burroughs High School in Burbank, California. At fifteen, he decided to take a break from acting to play basketball on the school team. He was getting playtime and he thought he had a chance to be a starter. "It meant turning down work, and that's almost heresy if you're an actor," he said. "But I was really committed to being on the team."[1]

He also began making films again. He had set

aside his eight-millimeter camera for a while, but when he was fifteen he decided to get back to it. "By the time I was sixteen, I was obsessed," he recalled. "I'd bully my little brother and his friends to be in all my movies."[2]

One of his films was about a boy who wandered onto a movie studio lot and imagined he was in the Old West. It placed second in a national Kodak film contest.

During his junior year in high school, Ronny became infatuated with the pretty, redheaded girl who sat in front of him in English class. Her name was Cheryl Alley. "She wasn't a cheerleader or popular in high school, and neither was I," he noted.[3]

The two began spending a lot of time together. Ronny's parents did not think that was a good idea. They said Ronny and Cheryl were too young for a steady relationship. Ronny came up with a plan to spend more time with Cheryl without his parents' knowing about it. He told them he was going out for the track team. When his parents thought he was at track practice, he was actually spending time with Cheryl.

Ronny was also co-editor of his high school's newspaper. "It was a chance to write, and I really got into it and loved it," he said.[4] He thought that if acting and directing did not work out for him, he might consider a career in journalism.

His backup career plan was not necessary. Ronny soon got a chance to be in another television series, *The Smith Family*. That series made its debut on January 20, 1971. Henry Fonda stars as a Los Angeles police detective. Ronny plays his teenage son.

That same year Ronny starred in a Disney Western called *The Wild Country*. It is about a family of four from Pittsburgh, Pennsylvania, who move west to Wyoming. Ronny and Clint Howard play the two sons.

Unfortunately, *The Smith Family* did not do well in the television ratings. In January 1972, the show was taken off the regular weekly lineup. A few more episodes of *The Smith Family* were shown between April and June 1972. Then the series went off the air for good.

Working on that series gave Ronny a chance to get acquainted with Henry Fonda, who gave him some advice about directing. Fonda saw one of Ronny's films and said, "You should do something with that, boy."[5] He also gave Ronny a copy of a book on film-making, *The Cinematographer's Manual*.

Ronny had also worked on a pilot episode for another television series. Writer/producer Garry Marshall came up with the idea for a series about a family living in the 1950s. In the pilot episode, "New Family in Town," the family is the first in the neighborhood to get a television set. It stars Ronny Howard, with Marion Ross as his mother.

They made only one episode, the pilot, and then the idea was shelved. Network executives said that no one cared about the fifties. In February 1972, that episode, renamed "Love and the Happy Day," was shown as a segment in the television series *Love American Style*. That airing helped the network earn back some of the cost of the making the pilot, but there was still no interest in making "Love and the Happy Day" into a series.

Ronny Howard with his father, Rance, and his brother, Clint. Ronny and Clint Howard played brothers in the movie The Wild Country.

Howard graduated from Burroughs High School in 1972. He then enrolled in the film program at the University of Southern California (USC). For a while he lived in a college dorm. Later, he got his own apartment near his parents' home.

In the meantime, "Love and the Happy Day" had attracted the attention of a young director named George Lucas. Lucas would later become famous for his *Star Wars* movies. But in 1972, at age twenty-eight, Lucas was just getting started in the moviemaking business. He had directed only one feature film, the science-fiction movie *THX 1138*, which was released in 1971.

Lucas was working on an idea for a film about teenagers growing up in the fifties. He was thinking about casting Ronny Howard in that film. He asked for a copy of "Love and the Happy Day" to get an idea of how Howard did in that type of role. He liked what he saw, so for his second film, *American Graffiti*, he cast Howard.

American Graffiti is about one night in the lives of four teenage boys. It is the last night of summer for the recent high school graduates. The four friends include John, the street drag racer; Curt, the serious one; Terry, the nerd; and Steve, the boy-next-door and senior class president, who is played by Howard.

Howard was the most familiar name in the cast, but several young actors and actresses got their start in that movie. Richard Dreyfuss plays the role of Curt. Harrison Ford appears as Bob Falta, a young man who challenges John to a drag race. Dreyfuss and Ford both went on to become major film stars.

Cindy Williams plays Steve's girlfriend, Laurie. Twelve-year-old Mackenzie Phillips is a pesky little girl who spends the evening riding around with John. Both went on to become stars in television series— Williams as Shirley in *Laverne and Shirley* and Phillips as the older daughter in *One Day at a Time*. Suzanne Somers makes a brief appearance as the mystery blonde in a white Chevy Thunderbird. She later starred in several television series, including *Three's Company*, *She's the Sheriff*, and *Step by Step*. The roles of John and Terry are played by Paul LeMat and Charles Martin Smith.

The setting for the movie is Modesto, California, in 1962. The film is filled with images of the time period from the late 1950s to the early 1960s. The teens gather at the local drive-in, where carhops on roller skates serve cherry Cokes, hamburgers, and fries.

When the teenagers are not at the drive-in, they are cruising around in their cars with their AM radios tuned to the local radio station. Songs like "Rock Around the Clock" and "Teen Angel" fill the night. There is also the chatter of the radio disc jockey known as Wolfman. That part is played by real-life disc jockey Wolfman Jack.

The movie was shot in twenty-eight days—actually twenty-eight nights. Since most of the action takes place at night, almost the entire movie was shot between 9:00 P.M. and 5:00 A.M.

For Howard, it was a chance to learn about filmmaking from Lucas. He asked questions and used his own camera, a Super-8, to film Lucas at work. "I bugged him like crazy," Howard later said. "He liked it, though."[6]

American Graffiti was released in August 1973. It received five Academy Award nominations, including Best Director and Best Picture. Although it did not win any Academy Awards, it was a hit with both audiences and critics. One critic called it "one of the best American films about adolescence ever made."[7] In *The New York Times* Stephen Farber noted: "George Lucas's *American Graffiti* is easily the best movie so far this year."[8]

Howard also starred in another movie, a horror film, released a couple of weeks after *American Graffiti. Happy Mother's Day, Love George* is set in New England. Howard plays Johnny, a young man who returns to his hometown to search for the father he never knew. When Johnny learns that his father was murdered, he begins a search for the killer.

For that movie, Howard dropped the name Ronny and was billed with the more adult-sounding Ron Howard. Howard had wanted to change his name for *American Graffiti*, but he did not tell Lucas in time. The film credits were already printed.

The success of *American Graffiti* and the Broadway musical *Grease*, also about the fifties, convinced television network executives that people were interested in that time period after all. They contacted Garry Marshall, who pulled "Love and the Happy Day" off the shelf and reworked it. It finally became a series titled *Happy Days*. The first show was televised on January 15, 1974. Ron Howard stars as Richie Cunningham, a high school junior from Milwaukee, Wisconsin.

4

Happy Days

*H*appy Days is about Richie Cunningham and his teenage problems with his friends, family, and school. Howard was nineteen years old when the series premiered. He had already graduated from high school, but he remembered having problems similar to Richie's when he was in school, especially Richie's shyness with girls. "They [girls] didn't throw themselves in my direction. . . . I was going through the same kind of nervous anxiety that Richie goes through all the time on *Happy Days*," he recalled.[1]

Some of Howard's own interests were also written into the *Happy Days* scripts. For example, Richie, like Howard, worked on his school newspaper.

Regulars on the series include Anson Williams as Richie's friend Potsie, and Marion Ross as Richie's mother. They had played those roles in the pilot episode, "Love and the Happy Day." Tom Bosley, who was not in the pilot, was hired for the part of Richie's father, Howard Cunningham. Donny Most plays Richie's friend Ralph Malph, and Erin Moran stars as Richie's younger sister, Joanie. Richie also has an older brother, Chuck, who was later written out of the series.

There is also a character named Arthur Fonzarelli played by Henry Winkler. He is better known as Fonzie or "the Fonz." He is a likable hoodlum who wears a leather jacket and rides a motorcycle. That character was created as a contrast to nice-guy Richie Cunningham. At first, it was a small part and Winkler's name was not even included in the opening credits.

The premiere of the show did well in the ratings. In a review for the *Washington Post*, Lawrence Laurent wrote: "The early indications, then, are that *Happy Days* will be around for a while and the biggest reason for its survival is . . . the skill of the oldest young professional performer in television, Ron Howard."[2]

There were also bad reviews. Some reviewers thought the series lacked depth because it did not deal with serious subjects. Howard agreed that some of the material was corny and said he never understood the show's success. On the other hand, he also realized that the show was meant to entertain, and it did.

Working on another television series did not give Howard much time for college. He left USC after four

Ron Howard and Tom Bosley in a scene from Happy Days. *Howard starred as Richie Cunningham in the series. Bosley played Richie's father.*

semesters. He thought he could learn just as much about directing on the job. In fact, Garry Marshall, the producer of *Happy Days*, wanted his young stars to learn about other areas of show business. He knew that with so many young people on the show, he had to find ways to keep them from getting bored. "I encouraged them to do other things—write something, look through the camera, anything else that interested them," Marshall said.[3]

Another way Marshall attempted to keep his stars happy was to try to make them feel like a family. He organized a softball team called the Happy Days All-Stars. On weekends, the All-Stars traveled around the country playing exhibition games in major-league baseball stadiums. The money they raised at these events went to charity. The games gave the cast a chance to meet their fans and also have fun with other cast members.

Occasionally, the games caused problems for the show's writers. An example was after a game in San Diego. During the game, Howard slid into home head-first while racing to beat a throw to home plate. He ended up with a black eye. The writers then had to invent an explanation for his injury in the episode they were filming that week.

Howard also worked on other projects. In 1974, he appeared on the big screen again in a Western, *The Spike's Gang*. It stars Lee Marvin as an outlaw who tries to turn three farm boys into bank robbers. Howard is Les Richter, one of the boys. Charles Martin Smith, who starred with Howard in *American Graffiti*, was cast as another of the farm boys.

Friends from Happy Days. *Pictured, left to right, are Donny Most as Ralph, Henry Winkler as Fonzie, Anson Williams as Potsie, and Howard as Richie Cunningham.*

The film was unimpressive. In a review for *The New York Times*, Vincent Canby noted that the movie failed to hold its audiences' attention. "During something as basic as a chase one's mind is likely to notice the cloud coverings," he wrote.[4]

In 1974, Howard starred in two television movies—*The Migrants* and *Locusts*. The following year, he had the title role in a television version of Mark Twain's *Huckleberry Finn*.

On June 7, 1975, Howard married his high school sweetheart, Cheryl Alley. At that time, she was a student at Cal State-Northridge. She later earned a bachelor's degree in psychology from that university. They agreed that they would postpone having children as long as Howard was on *Happy Days*. "You can work and be a parent—but not at this pace," Howard explained.[5]

By the third season of *Happy Days*, the emphasis of the show shifted. Fonzie, played by Henry Winkler, was a big hit with television audiences. As his popularity grew, the show's ratings soared. Network executives decided to make his role larger. The show began to focus more on Fonzie's problems than on Richie's.

Howard admitted that he felt awkward about that change at first, but it did not cause problems on the set. "Maybe if Henry Winkler and I hadn't liked each other . . . there would have been problems," Howard said.[6] He also thought that Winkler's popularity helped make the show a success, and that was good for everyone involved with the series.

As a child, Howard had seen the same thing happen on another series—*The Andy Griffith Show*.

Andy Griffith is the star of that series, but it was comedian Don Knotts in the role of Deputy Barney Fife who got all the attention. Knotts won five Emmy awards for his role as Barney, but it took both characters to make that series work. It was the same with *Happy Days*.

On the other hand, when there was talk about changing the name of the show to *Fonzie's Happy Days*, Howard took a stand. He said he "didn't sign on to be on somebody else's show."[7] Garry Marshall, the show's producer, agreed with Howard and the idea was dropped.

In 1975, Howard married his high school sweetheart, Cheryl Alley. Pictured here with them at the wedding are members of the Happy Days *cast, including, from left, Donny Most, Anson Williams, and Tom Bosley.*

As a member of the *Happy Days* cast, Howard was expected to go on publicity tours. When the cast made an appearance somewhere, such as at a mall, thousands of enthusiastic fans turned out to see them. Howard was not comfortable being mobbed by fans. He began to think more about becoming a director. He saw directing as a chance to work in a business he loved without being so visible to his fans.

He talked to his wife about making a change. "I bet if I actually pulled this thing off and became a director, this would die down pretty quickly," he said.[8]

She told him to give it a try.

Howard soon got a chance to take a step in that direction. Producer Roger Corman of New World Pictures wanted Howard to star in his new movie, *Eat My Dust*. Corman was the king of low-budget action movies featuring car chases and crash scenes. It was not the type of movie Howard wanted to do. "I hated *Eat My Dust*, hated the script," he later said, "but from my film-school days at USC I knew that Roger Corman was like a ray of hope for student filmmakers. He was one guy who would take chances on directors."[9] They worked out an agreement that if Howard would star in *Eat My Dust*, Corman might give Howard a chance to direct a film.

Eat My Dust opened in theaters on May 28, 1976, with Howard starring as a teenager named Hoover. He tries to impress a girl by stealing a stock car from a local racetrack. This sets off a car chase involving twenty-seven vehicles.

Eat My Dust was a hit with drive-in movie

audiences. It grossed $18 million and gave investors a 400 percent return on their money.

Later that year, Howard starred with John Wayne in *The Shootist*. In that film, Wayne plays J. B. Books, an old shootist, or gunslinger. The movie is about the last days of his life. Books moves into the widow Rogers' boardinghouse to live out what time he has left. Howard plays her son, Gillam, who sees Books as a hero.

"I went into the movie expecting I wouldn't have a good time doing it," Howard recalled. "John Wayne was notorious for not getting along with young actors."[10]

As it turned out, Howard enjoyed working with Wayne. "I was 21 years old at the time and he always called me 'old 21' on the set," Howard remembered fondly. "He never ever made me feel like a kid."[11] When they were not busy shooting, Wayne and Howard played chess. Wayne usually won those games.

Howard was nominated for a Golden Globe award as best supporting actor for his role in *The Shootist*. In the meantime, Roger Corman stuck to his agreement to give Howard a chance. Howard was about to direct his first movie.

Getting a Start

Roger Corman was very specific about the type of movie he wanted from Howard. The film would be a car-chase comedy titled *Grand Theft Auto*. Corman also said that the movie had to have a PG (Parental Guidance) rating and Howard had to star in it.

Grand Theft Auto was not the kind of movie Howard dreamed of directing. He was more interested in developing characters. On the other hand, Roger Corman's New World Pictures had served as a training ground for some of America's top filmmakers. Howard knew that if he wanted to get a start as a director, he had to take advantage of opportunities like the one Corman was giving him.

The odds were against Howard's succeeding as a director. Few have been successful in making the leap from television actor to Hollywood director. Howard welcomed the challenge. He said that as an actor he sometimes felt helpless. If he did not like a script or the way a scene was edited, there was nothing he could do because he did not have control. As the director, he would be in charge. "It's one of the reasons why I wanted to become a director," he explained.[1]

Even so, Howard was nervous about directing his first film. One of his concerns was the budget. Filmmakers keep the costs down on low-budget movies like *Grand Theft Auto* by shooting them in only a few days. Howard knew that Corman expected him to work fast, so he did his homework.

Before filming began, he diagrammed all the shots for the movie. He then made a schedule of how many scenes he would film each day. He planned to use two camera-setup crews to meet that schedule.

Howard started filming on March 2, 1977. Halfway through the first day, he began to panic because he was already behind schedule. "The first day I had to do thirty setups," he recalled. "Halfway through the morning, I'd gotten through four. I walked off and thought, 'Forget directing.'"[2]

Fortunately, things got better. Howard was able to complete the movie in twenty-two days. One day of shooting included ninety-one camera setups. "That's a record for the most setups in any movie," he stated proudly.[3]

In the movie, Howard plays the role of Sam

Freeman, a middle-class teenager who is in love with Paula Powers, the daughter of a millionaire business-man. Nancy Morgan plays the role of Paula.

Paula's parents want her to marry Collins Hedgeworth, the proper young man they have picked out for her. She wants to marry Sam. Her father refuses to give her permission, so Paula and Sam decide to elope. They take off for Las Vegas in her father's Rolls-Royce. When Paula's father discovers she is gone, he offers a reward for her return. Friends, relatives, private detectives, ministers, mobsters, a chicken farmer, a radio disc jockey, and the police pursue the couple in a chase that makes up most of the movie.

The chase scenes involve a variety of vehicles, including vans, helicopters, highway patrol cars, a racecar, and a bus full of elderly people on a church outing. Marion Ross, Richie Cunningham's mother on *Happy Days*, plays the part of Collins Hedgeworth's mother. She also gets into the race chasing after her son, who is pursuing Paula and Sam. Finally, the couple lands in the middle of a demolition derby.

The movie was a family affair for the Howards. Ron Howard and his father, Rance, wrote the screenplay. Both Rance and Clint Howard have parts in the film. When the crew complained that they were tired of eating fast food, Cheryl Howard began cooking for them. She prepared meals for the eighty-five-member crew during the last eleven days of filming.

Howard shot the movie at a cost of $602,000, and it grossed $15 million at the box office. Critics said the movie compared favorably with other films of that

Ron Howard and Nancy Morgan in a scene from the movie Grand Theft Auto. *Howard directed and starred in the movie as Sam Freeman. Nancy Morgan played Sam's girlfriend, Paula Powers. It was the first movie Howard directed.*

type. In *The New York Times*, Lawrence Van Gelder wrote: "Nobody who has ever wanted to see a Rolls-Royce in a demolition derby is going to walk away from this movie disappointed."[4]

Howard then reported for work on his fifth season of *Happy Days*. He had another two years left on his contract and he intended to honor it. "I like the people I'm working with, and it's really only a forty-hour week, so I can work on a lot of other projects," he said.[5]

Although Howard was paid well for his work on *Happy Days*, he and his wife lived simply. They bought a home in a modest neighborhood not far from where *Happy Days* was filmed. Howard drove to work in a Volkswagen van. Their idea of a good time was an evening at home watching old movies on television. A night out was attending a Los Angeles Dodgers baseball game.

Roger Corman wanted to do another film with Howard, but Howard had reached an agreement with the NBC television network to do a movie for it. That movie, *Cotton Candy*, was a story that had been in the back of Howard's mind for a while.

Ron and Clint Howard worked on the script together. They talked about what they wanted, but because Ron Howard was busy with *Happy Days*, Clint got the job of actually putting the words down on paper. The brothers had regular meetings to go over the scenes and discuss what needed to be changed. Then Clint Howard made the revisions.

Part of the movie was filmed in Los Angeles and the rest was done on location at Lake Highland High

School in Dallas, Texas. By the time they started filming, Howard was on hiatus from *Happy Days*. He had grown a mustache, and he showed up in Dallas wearing sunglasses and a hat. His disguise did not fool the students who crowded around him asking for autographs. Howard said that he would send autographed photos to anyone who left an address. In two days, there were more than six thousand requests.

Not all of Howard's fans were satisfied with an autographed photo. One evening a fan crept in during a supper break and stole Howard's leftovers right off his plate. "I can understand somebody grabbing my hat," he said. "But my chicken bones?"[6]

Many people thought of Howard as being like the characters he played on *The Andy Griffith Show* and *Happy Days*—shy and willing to please. They wondered if he was tough enough to be a director. Charles Martin Smith said he was.

Smith, who played Terry in *American Graffiti*, also stars in *Cotton Candy*. He noted that Howard had great confidence when he was directing. "Ron can't make a decision about where to go for dinner, but he had an answer for everybody on the set. It was amazing," Smith said. "He was totally in control."[7]

Howard's mother, Jean, plays the part of a teacher in *Cotton Candy*. His father is the vice-principal of the school. Clint Howard plays one of the teenagers, and Cheryl Howard appears as his prom date. Ron Howard makes a cameo appearance as a rock star.

Howard's mother joked about the reason they were all in the film. There was a clause in Howard's contract that said that if he went over budget, he would have to pay the extra costs out of his own money. "It's hard to undercut our price," she quipped.[8]

That was not the only reason they were all in the film. Howard says he likes working with his family. Perhaps that is because show business has always been a family business for the Howards.

Howard completed *Cotton Candy* ahead of schedule and stayed under the $1.1 million budget. The crew then celebrated with a wrap party that included a cream pie fight between the Los Angeles and Dallas location crews. Howard joined in on the fun.

Howard returned to acting on the big screen with a sequel to *American Graffiti* called *More American Graffiti*. It was released in 1979. The movie features most of the original characters, continuing their story in the 1970s.

Steve and Laurie, again played by Howard and Cindy Williams, are a married couple living in the suburbs. The story line centers on a conflict over Laurie's decision to get a job—a subject that movie audiences found ho-hum. The film played to mostly empty theaters. A reviewer for *Newsweek* summed up the public's feelings about the sequel when he wrote: "'More' in this case is decidedly less."[9]

After seven and a half years on *Happy Days*, Howard left the series when his contract was up in 1980. He wanted to devote more time to directing, but he admitted that leaving the show was a scary decision. "It was leaving behind a way of life, and a salary level, and really committing to something unknown at that point," he said.[10]

Happy Days continued for another three and a half years without the character of Richie. The writers explained his absence by having Richie graduate from college, join the army, and get shipped off to Greenland.

In September 1980, Howard starred in another television movie, *Act of Love.* He plays a young man charged in the mercy killing of his brother, who is paralyzed as the result of a motorcycle accident. Critics praised Howard's performance in that role.

The idea for the next movie that Howard directed came from Anson Williams, who played Richie's friend Potsie on *Happy Days.* Howard and Williams were co-producers of that television movie, *Skyward.*

The movie is about a teenager whose spine was damaged. She would never walk again, but she day-dreams about flying like a bird. She becomes friends with the airport café owner who is a former stunt pilot. Film legend Bette Davis stars in that role. Howard Hesseman plays a loner who is rebuilding an old bi-wing airplane. Davis teaches the girl to fly in Hesseman's plane.

Ron Howard admitted that he was nervous about directing Bette Davis. She was then seventy-two years old and had a reputation for not being very patient with young film directors. Howard was only twenty-six years old.

Howard said Davis tested him on the set at first. He asked her to call him Ron, but she refused. "I'll call you Mr. Howard until I decide if I like you or not," she said.[11]

One day, Howard asked Davis to do a scene in a

particular way. She did not like his idea, but she did it the way he wanted. When the scene turned out well, Davis admitted that Howard knew what he was doing. "You're absolutely right," she said. "That makes the scene."[12]

After that, she called him Ron.

Howard and Williams both believed that it would bring more honesty to the film to have an actual wheelchair user play the part of the girl with the spinal injury. Suzy Gilstrap, a fourteen-year-old paraplegic, made her acting debut in that role. Marion Ross plays her overprotective mother.

While Howard was working on *Skyward* at Paramount Studios, he met a producer named Brian Grazer. At the time, Grazer was executive producer for several television pilots. Howard and the twenty-nine-year-old Grazer were the two youngest people with offices at Paramount.

One day over lunch, Grazer told Howard about an idea he had for a movie. It came from a newspaper article about two men in New York City who were running a prostitution ring out of the city's morgue. Grazer wondered if Howard would be interested in directing a movie based on that idea.

"I kind of liked it but didn't flip over it," Howard recalled.[13] However, he said he would be interested if the script was funny. Lowell Ganz and Babaloo Mandel, who had been writers for *Happy Days*, were hired to write the screenplay. In the meantime, Howard worked on other projects.

"Opie Cunningham"

Ron and Cheryl Howard had postponed having children until Howard was finished with *Happy Days*. Now they were ready to start a family. Their daughter Bryce was born in 1981.

Howard admits that he is a workaholic, but he said becoming a father made him more conscious of the fact that he needed to take time to relax and enjoy his family. Still, with all the projects he had going, it did not appear that he was taking any time off.

Howard had a hand in three television movies that were shown in 1981. In May, he starred in *Bitter Harvest*. It is based on a true story from the midseventies about a midwestern dairy farmer who discovers that a toxic chemical known as PPB was mistakenly mixed with cattle feed. In a review for *TV Guide*, Judith Crist wrote that Howard's performance as the young farmer was "first-rate."[1]

In November, Howard starred with Buddy Ebsen in *Fire on the Mountain*. In that movie, Ebsen is an old-timer who takes on the U.S. Army. The army wants to build a missile site on Ebsen's land, but he refuses to sell the property. Howard is a young man who comes back to town hoping to make money in real estate on the deal. He ends up siding with the old man.

Howard also directed a two-part movie called *Through the Magic Pyramid*, which was televised in December. Rance Howard and Herbert J. Wright wrote the script for that movie about an eleven-year-old boy who travels back in time to ancient Egypt. His mission is to rescue the future King Tut from kidnappers.

Television movies gave Howard a chance to play a variety of characters, but he felt he was limited as an actor. "I was doing lots of good TV movies, but there wasn't very much theatrical interest in me," he said. "I doubt that would have changed; I don't think that I would have been an important part of the movie business as an actor."[2]

Howard believed he would have better opportunities as a director, and he was already at work directing his second feature film. Ganz and Mandel had completed the screenplay for *Night Shift*, the story about two men who run a prostitution ring out of the New York City morgue.

Henry Winkler was cast in the role of Chuck

Lumley, a nerdy worker on the night shift at the morgue. It was a contrast to his supercool Fonzie character on *Happy Days*. His co-stars in the movie were two unknowns—Shelley Long, as one of the prostitutes, and Michael Keaton, as Bill Blazejowski, Chuck's co-worker at the morgue.

Night Shift was released in September 1982 with an R (Restricted) rating. That was no surprise, considering the subject matter. Other reasons for the rating included partial nudity and bad language. Howard seemed to be sending a message that he was not going to make children's films.

The movie got mixed reviews. Howard noted that critics on the West Coast liked it, but in New York City, reviewers were divided. The movie never really caught on in theaters. That was discouraging for Howard because most people who saw the movie liked it. "We never had a bad screening of *Night Shift*," he noted.[3]

The movie eventually found an audience on cable television and in video rentals. It also launched the careers of Michael Keaton and Shelley Long. Keaton went on to play the title role in the movie *Batman*. Long starred as Diane Chambers in the hit television series *Cheers*.

Although Howard was now spending his time behind the camera, he could not escape the fame he had achieved as a star of two television series. After the release of *Night Shift*, he was the guest host on the television show *Saturday Night Live*. On that show, he appeared in a skit with actor/comedian Eddie Murphy, who played Raheem the Film Critic.

In the skit, Murphy/Raheem introduced Howard as "Opie Cunningham." Then Murphy tried to shave off Howard's mustache. (During his years on *Happy Days*, Howard sometimes grew a mustache after filming ended for the season. But he had to shave it off for his role as Richie when each new season began.) In the *Saturday Night Live* sketch, Howard protested: "I'm a director now. I've got a movie out called *Night Shift*."[4]

After that show, people on the street started calling him Opie Cunningham. Howard admitted that at one time it bothered him that people continued to remember him mainly as the two characters he played in television series.[5] On the other hand, he realized that when people called him Opie, Richie, or Opie Cunningham, they were just kidding around: "Most of them are pretty much up to date on who I really am."[6]

Howard had been finishing up work on *Night Shift* when Brian Grazer told him about an idea he had for a story about a mermaid. Howard read the script written by Bruce Jay Friedman, but he was not very excited about it. For one thing, he was not sure that he wanted to do another comedy right away. He also thought the characters spent too much time under water.

Then Howard began thinking of the script as a love story. One of the changes he suggested was to have more of the action take place on land. He also wanted to tell the story from the man's point of view. Lowell Ganz and Babaloo Mandel did a script rewrite for the movie titled *Splash*.

Howard and Grazer ran into a snag when they tried to find a studio to finance the movie. Studio heads thought the story about a produce merchant from Manhattan who falls in love with a mermaid was too silly. Disney was interested, but Howard hesitated. He thought the Howard/Disney combination sounded a little too cute.

"It seemed just too perfect," he said. "Little Ronny Howard grows up to make films for Walt Disney studios. That bothered me." [7] But he did not have much of a choice. Disney was the only studio willing to take a chance on the movie.

Howard directs a scene from Splash, *a story about a man who falls in love with a mermaid. Brian Grazer, far left, was the producer of the movie.*

Tom Hanks was cast in the role of the lonely bachelor who runs the family produce business. Hanks had starred in a television series called *Bosom Buddies*, but this was his film debut. John Candy was recruited to play the part of Hanks's playboy brother. Candy had appeared in seventeen films over five years, but always in small roles. This was his first big part. Darryl Hannah got the part of the mermaid, even though Howard did not believe the story she told him at her audition.

Hannah told Howard that as a child growing up in Chicago, she sometimes pretended that she was a mermaid. She said that she would tie her feet together, put on fins, and swim around the family's pool. Howard did not care if her story was true or not. He was not concerned about her swimming ability. He planned to use a body double for the underwater scenes anyway. In moviemaking, a *body double* is someone who physically resembles the actor and may be photographed in scenes where no face is shown.

Howard did ask Hannah to get in the water and swim around a bit. He wanted to get an idea for size and shape for her body double. Once he saw her swim, he knew that she had been telling the truth. In the end, Howard used a body double for Hannah in only one scene.

Swimming may have been the easiest part for Hannah. Getting dressed in the thirty-five-pound mermaid tail was the hard part. It took technicians three hours each day to get her into the form-fitting mermaid costume. "At lunch they'd yank me out on a crane and plop me on the deck," she said.[8] When they finished filming for the day, technicians cut the fin away from her body.

Filming underwater presented a few challenges. One of the challenges for Howard was just getting used to the water. Although he grew up in California, he never spent a lot of time swimming in the ocean. "I just don't care much for water," Howard told a reporter.[9] Part of his preparation for the movie was to learn to scuba dive.

Howard set up an underwater lifeline for the actors to use during filming. As soon as Hannah and Hanks finished a scene, they swam over to the lifeline for oxygen. Sometimes it was a struggle just to keep the actors in front of the camera. They tended to get pushed right out of a scene by the strong ocean currents.

Howard appeared to have an answer for every problem that came up during filming. That was no surprise to Hanks, who respected Howard's years in show business. "He has seen absolutely everything that can possibly happen on a set, because the man started doing it three months before he was born or something like that," Hanks joked.[10]

Once again Howard cast members of his family in the movie. Rance Howard plays a produce customer who complained about the service. Clint and Cheryl Howard appear as guests at a wedding. Even the writers, Lowell Ganz and Babaloo Mandel, have small parts in the movie.

Most of the reviews for *Splash* were positive. Richard Schickel, a critic for *Time* magazine, recommended the movie. He urged audiences to "take a plunge on *Splash*."[11] In a review for the *New Yorker*, Pauline Kael wrote: "Ron Howard has a happy touch, and he's the first film director who has let John Candy loose."[12]

One of Howard's strengths as a director is that he gets along with actors and wants their ideas. "I see myself as more of an editor of their ideas, rather than a person who only executes his own ideas," Howard said.[13]

Splash was a hit at the box office and was a turning point for Howard as a director. It gave him something known in the entertainment business as leverage. It meant that he was now being taken seriously. Studios were interested in making movies that he wanted to direct. Critic David Ansen summed up this change in a review he wrote for *Newsweek*. "After *Splash*, anyone who smirks at the notion that little Opie is a filmmaker is going to look like a fool."[14]

The movie also established Tom Hanks's career. When other actors saw what Howard did for Hanks, they wanted to work with Howard too.

Producers Richard Zanuck and David Brown saw *Splash* and wanted Howard to direct a movie they were doing titled *Cocoon*. "We were impressed by him, but it was not easy to get him," Brown recalled.[15]

"From Tyke to Tycoon"

Cocoon is about a group of elderly people living in a retirement community in Florida. For fun, they sneak into a nearby abandoned mansion to swim in the estate's indoor pool. Then a couple rents the mansion. The elderly people continue to use the pool when the renters are not home, only now large, strange-looking pods, or cocoons, begin to appear at the bottom of the pool. At the same time, the retired citizens begin to notice that they are feeling younger and healthier after swimming in the pool, which they now share with the cocoons. They soon discover that the change has something to do with aliens from outer space.

"When I was offered *Cocoon*, my first instinct was,

'Better not; just better not,'" Howard said.[1] He was concerned about comparisons that he knew would be made. First, there were the obvious comparisons to *Splash*. In both movies, water was important.

Second, *Cocoon* featured space aliens. There had already been two blockbuster alien movies, *Close Encounters of the Third Kind* (1977) and *E.T.: The Extraterrestrial* (1982). Steven Spielberg directed both of those movies. Howard did not feel that he was ready to be compared with Spielberg.[2]

He finally decided to take the job of directing *Cocoon* because he liked the characters. Also, he had not been able to get financing for a movie he wanted to do, titled *Old Friends*. That project was Cheryl Howard's idea. She was an aspiring screenwriter, and she and Howard wrote the script together. The story featured a love triangle involving three elderly characters.

Although Howard was not able to get financing for *Old Friends*, he liked the idea of doing a movie about senior citizens. He also liked the fact that all of the development had already been done on *Cocoon*. The film was going to be made. All he had to do was direct. He did ask for a rewrite on the script so that there was more emphasis on character and less on science fiction.

Cocoon was budgeted at about $18 million. It was the most expensive film Howard had worked on so far. Because of the alien theme, there were a lot of special effects. Howard knew that the way to learn was to ask questions. When he wanted advice about special effects, he went to an expert—Steven Spielberg.

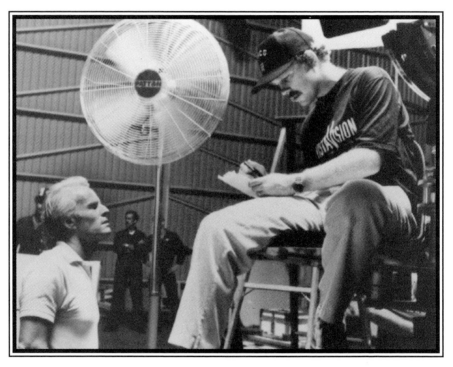

Howard talks with producer Richard Zanuck on the set of the movie Cocoon.

Spielberg had sent Howard a note congratulating him on his success with *Splash*. The two directors met for lunch in Los Angeles, and Howard got Spielberg's advice about some of the special effects he wanted to use.

The movie's cast includes a group of veteran actors: Don Ameche, Wilford Brimley, Maureen Stapleton, Gwen Verdon, Jack Gilford, Hume Cronyn, and Jessica Tandy. Some of them had been in show business longer than Howard had been alive.

Howard was not worried about directing them. He remembered his experience directing Bette Davis a few years earlier. That turned out well and it gave him the confidence he needed for directing the stars of *Cocoon*.

The cast of *Cocoon* did not appear to be concerned that Howard was so young. "He seems like he's been doing it [directing] for years," Maureen Stapleton noted.[3]

"I found he listened, and he wanted you to improvise, and I like that," Hume Cronyn said.[4]

More important, they all noted that it was fun to work with Howard. "His was the most relaxed set I've ever seen," one cast member said.[5] Other actors who have worked with Howard agree.

Howard likes a calm set, but he admits that he does not always feel as relaxed as he appears.[6] When Clint Howard works with his brother, he tries to help him relax. "A lot of times I'll see Ron not having fun on the set. And I'll start joking around, shadow boxing with him, telling jokes at his cost, you know, ragging on him . . . little things to lighten things up," he explained.[7]

Clint Howard plays the role of an employee of the retirement center in *Cocoon*. Howard's parents also have small parts. Hundreds of senior citizens worked as extras in the film, which was shot on various locations in Florida. Jean Howard is an extra in a scene with a group of elderly people on a boat waiting to meet up with a space ship. Rance Howard plays the role of a detective.

Howard took his wife and children with him to

Howard and cast members from Cocoon *share a laugh on the set. From left: Maureen Stapleton, Don Ameche, Hume Cronyn, and Jessica Tandy.*

New York for the premiere of the movie in June 1985. The family had grown in the last few months to include twin daughters, Jocelyn and Paige. They were four months old when *Cocoon* was released. Howard's eldest daughter, Bryce, was four years old.

At the premiere, Howard slipped into the theater forty-five minutes after the film began. He left quietly before it was over. He has said that one of his greatest joys as a director is to sit in a darkened theater and watch how the audience responds to one of his films. "I'm an audience guy," he said. "I always hope to please the audience."[8]

Cocoon was a hit with audiences, but, according to David Brooks of the *Washington Post*, Howard was disappointed that he was not nominated for an Academy Award for that movie. "He'd better get used to it," Brooks wrote.[9] He observed that there was a prejudice against the type of movies Howard made—movies that were entertaining but not serious enough to win awards.

A month after the release of *Cocoon*, Howard began filming another movie, *Gung Ho*. That film, starring Michael Keaton, is about a Japanese auto manufacturer moving into a Pennsylvania town. The idea came from a segment on the television news show *60 Minutes* that had reported on a story about the opening of a *Nissan* auto plant in Smyrna, Tennessee.

Although the original topic was serious, *Gung Ho* was a comedy. "This project offered a great opportunity to be very funny and at the same time comment on something we're reading about every day," Howard said.[10] The humor comes from the cultural differences between the Japanese and American workers. The Japanese employees are portrayed as workaholics. The Americans, on the other hand, are more relaxed. They work hard, but they also take time to enjoy other things.

Howard knew he was dealing with sensitive material. He did not want to offend Japanese people. His success in walking that tightrope was shown when Japanese actor Soh Yamamura accepted a part in the movie.

Yamamura was seventy-five years old and a well-known actor in Japan, but he had been in very few American films. He had turned down roles because he did not like the way Japanese people were portrayed in American movies. He liked *Gung Ho*.

On the other hand, at least one movie reviewer found something troubling about the movie. He criticized Howard for his choice of location for filming. He noted that although the film appeared to praise American workers, Howard spent three weeks filming at a factory in Argentina in South America, instead of using a U.S. factory. "Howard himself is guilty of a strange kind of hypocrisy," the reviewer wrote.[11]

Gung Ho was released in March 1986. The following month, Howard made a brief return to acting, starring as a grown-up Opie Taylor in the television movie *Return to Mayberry*.

In that movie, Andy Taylor returns to Mayberry to run for sheriff. Opie is the editor of the local newspaper.

He is married to a woman named Eunice and they are expecting their first baby.

Frances Bavier was too sick to return as Aunt Bee. Clint Howard also missed the reunion show because he was working on another movie. Most of the rest of the cast did return. "I think everybody would have been disappointed not to be asked," Howard said.[12]

On the other hand, he admitted that he had doubts about returning to his old role. He was afraid it would change his memories of the people he worked with as a child. "As a kid, I loved those people," he said.[13]

As it turned out, he did not need to worry. "It was great—exactly the same as I remembered," he said. "If anything, as an adult I like the people even more. . . . They taught me a lot about professionalism. And about normal, decent behavior."[14]

Howard celebrated his thirty-second birthday on the set. The cast presented him with a cake.

Return to Mayberry was broadcast on NBC-TV on April 13, 1986. It got a fifty-three share in the Nielson ratings. That meant that more than half the people in the United States who were watching television at that time were tuned in to the movie.

While Howard was revisiting his old neighborhood in Mayberry, he was moving out of his real-life neighborhood. Howard said he and his wife wanted to move to a place where show business was not so important in people's lives. "I'm very happy about the way I grew up," he noted, "but I want my kids to know there are people who do things besides make movies and TV shows."[15]

The Howard family moved into a seven-bedroom, colonial-style home in Greenwich, Connecticut. The house had a vegetable garden and a fenced-in area for their animals—including one sheep, two African pygmy goats, and two dogs. They also had house pets—a guinea pig, a parakeet, a snake, and two cats.

Ron and Cheryl Howard had already decided that their children would have a normal life away from public view. They do not allow their children to be photographed for publication, and they are against letting them become child stars. "I wouldn't allow them to be kid actors, knowing what I know," Howard said.[16]

What he knows is that many child stars have problems later in life. They experience great success early in their lives, but when they get older they have trouble finding work in other shows. Many turn to drugs or alcohol in an attempt to ease their disappointment.

Howard said it was different for him for a couple of reasons. First of all, his parents made sure that he had a normal life away from the set. Second, his dad was there to teach him how to act. Howard said many child actors are trained to play one role. When they are done with that role, their careers are finished because they have not learned anything about acting. On the other hand, when Howard was done being Opie, he could go on to other roles because his dad had taught him how to be an actor.

Howard also noted that his dad was on the set with him when he was working. That took a lot of time, and it was something Ron and Cheryl Howard were not willing to do. Howard said that if he or his wife were to spend months supervising one of their children on a television or movie set, it would be very unfair to their other children.

Although Howard now lived in Connecticut, he was still very much a part of the Hollywood scene. He and producer Brian Grazer teamed up to form their own film company, Imagine Films Entertainment. They planned to develop film and television projects and then find studios to finance them. Howard said one of the main reasons he wanted to form his own company was that it would make it easier for him to do the movies he wanted to do.

Howard and Grazer had worked on several films together before they officially became partners. They planned to continue the same working relationship. Grazer made the deals. "I call the agents, the lawyers, the business managers," he said.[17] Howard concentrated on the creative part of the business.

Some people thought that Howard and Grazer divided their work in that way because Howard was not able to make the deals. He was just too nice a guy.

Howard's reputation as a nice guy began with his Opie Taylor and Richie Cunningham roles. Although they were only parts he played, the way he lived his life did not tarnish that image. He was, after all, a family man still married to his high school sweetheart. He got along with the people he worked with and had earned their respect.

One magazine reporter wrote a tongue-in-cheek article about how he had spent a night out on the town

Howard and his wife, Cheryl. The Howards moved to Greenwich, Connecticut, to raise their children out of the public eye. Howard says that although he had a good experience as a child actor, he does not want his children to follow in his footsteps.

with Howard trying to find something bad to write about him. The reporter came up empty-handed.

Howard did admit that at one time he tried to rebel against his nice guy image. "When I gave an interview, I'd act tough and I'd be sure to swear," he explained.[18]

His rebellion did not last long. "It really wasn't me," he said.[19]

On the other hand, people who believed that Howard could not make business deals because he was too nice were mistaken. "The whole 'nice' thing has been overplayed," said actor Michael Keaton, who worked for Howard in *Night Shift* and *Gung Ho*. "He can make cold, hard decisions when he needs to."[20]

Howard divided his time between his office in Los Angeles, where the business was based, and his home in Connecticut. He spent about two days a week in his office. When he was in Connecticut, he talked to Grazer by phone two or three times a day.

In August 1986, they went public with their company. It meant that anyone who wanted to invest in the company could buy shares in it. By selling stock in the company they were able to raise $13.3 million to operate the business. Howard and Grazer signed a six-year contract with their stockholders. "In the eyes of Wall Streeters, Ron Howard has made a successful transition from tyke to tycoon," a reporter for *Time* magazine wrote.[21]

Soon, Howard began working on his next movie, an extravagant fantasy titled *Willow*. The Howards also celebrated the birth of a son, Reed.

8

From Fantasy to Real Life

Howard had been working on an idea for a fantasy film, but the story was not coming together. He decided to ask his friend George Lucas for advice. Lucas had an idea of his own. He had first thought of it fifteen years earlier when he was doing research for his *Star Wars* movies. He asked Howard to work with him on that idea.

Lucas and Howard had many meetings during the next year to talk about the kind of movie they wanted to make. As with other Lucas films, there would be many special effects. Bob Dolman was hired to write the screenplay, and he also joined them at their meetings. Later, the illustrators hired to work on the special effects met with them. Howard says those meetings were a lot of fun, with everyone coming up with ideas based on their own childhood experiences.

As a child, Howard liked dinosaurs and he was fascinated with two-headed monsters. He also recalled stories that his dad had told him about a character named Tiny Tim, who had a magic tooth-pick. When he rubbed the toothpick, he would shrink until he was small enough to ride on the wing of a bird. "Tiny Tim was always going off into some fairy tale world roaming around solving a problem," Howard recalled.[1]

Howard and Lucas ended up with a story that included an evil queen, a princess, and a renegade warrior. There were also fairies, brownies, trolls, sorcerers, a two-headed fire-breathing monster, and a village of peace-loving little people called Nelwyns. Howard was the director and Lucas the producer of the movie that would be titled *Willow*.

The central character, Willow, was a Nelwyn. Warwick Davis, an eighteen-year-old, three-foot-four-inch English actor, plays that part. He previously appeared as Wicket in *Return of the Jedi* (1983), one of the *Star Wars* movies.

Davis dreamed of becoming a director, and he hoped to learn from watching Howard on the set. Howard enjoyed the irony of that situation. He was eighteen years old when he followed George Lucas around the set during the filming of *American Graffiti*.

One thing Howard learned from Lucas on the set of *American Graffiti* was that details were important. "The details work like glue to hold the movie together," Howard explained.[2]

There were many details to think about in filming *Willow*. The cast includes thousands of people who act as extras in big scenes. Filming was done in distant locations, such as England, Scotland, and New Zealand, and under difficult conditions, such as on top of a snowy mountain. Then there were the special effects. They were so complex that it sometimes took weeks just to film one scene. It took almost a year to do the whole movie. Cast members said that Howard managed to stay upbeat the whole time.

Val Kilmer, who plays Madmartigan the renegade warrior, said Howard was always enthusiastic during filming. "He had to be that way. It's his nature. . . . He's still Opie," Kilmer joked.[3]

Joanne Whalley, an English actress who later married Kilmer, plays the part of the evil queen's daughter. She noted how well Howard and Lucas worked together.

Howard admitted that he had some concerns about working with Lucas. Other directors complained that Lucas had trouble letting directors be in charge. They said he spent too much time on the set and that he sometimes interfered with their directing.

During the filming of *Willow*, Lucas was on the set about half the time. Howard said that most of the time he was happy to have him there. On the other hand, there were times when Lucas got too involved. Howard recalled the first time that happened. He pointed down at his toes and said, "George, you see these toes here? You're stepping on them a little bit." "Oh, sorry," Lucas answered.[4] Then he stepped aside to let Howard direct.

Howard took an active role in promoting the film. He appeared to enjoy talking with reporters, joking with them as he answered their questions. In the movie, a sorceress is transformed into several different talking animals. One reporter asked Howard how he got the little animals to talk. "I took 'em out to dinner a couple of times," he quipped.[5]

A toy merchandising campaign was planned to go along with the film. It included action figures of the main characters. Howard told a reporter that he did not get involved with that part of the production. "I asked them if there was going to be a Ron Howard action director doll. They told me no, so I lost interest," he joked.[6]

The one question Howard would not answer was how much it cost to make the movie. Unofficial sources estimated the cost to be about $35 million.[7]

Howard would not confirm that figure, and he used a baseball story to explain why. He recalled a time just after Pete Rose signed a high-salary contract with the Philadelphia Phillies. Rose made a bad play at first base during a game Howard attended. Immediately, a man behind Howard in the stands stood up and began shouting about all the money Rose earned, as if his salary meant that he wasn't allowed to make mistakes. "I thought, 'Wow—it all comes down to that, and that's not right,'" Howard said. "You shouldn't have to think about the money at the game."[8]

Unfortunately, *Willow* was not a hit in theaters. Critics said that it tried to appeal to too many age groups and there were too many subplots. They also

Howard holds young actress Dawn Downing on the set of Willow. *With them are producer George Lucas (center) and actor Warwick Davis, who played the role of Willow.*

thought there were too many special effects and that Howard did not do a good job of directing action scenes.

One reviewer wrote that Howard relied "too much on lavish swordplay, sorcery and galloping horses."[9] In a review for *Time* magazine, Richard Corliss noted, "Director Ron Howard gets the social politics of the dwarfs' village right, but he is not adept at action scenes: some are too busy; others are botched."[10]

Howard already knew that he wanted to do something simpler for his next movie. He wanted it to be a comedy with no special effects. It would also be about something important to him. "The thing I'm going through right now is all the changes that coincide with becoming a parent," he said.[11] That was the subject of his next movie, *Parenthood*.

Lowell Ganz and Babaloo Mandel, who worked with Howard on *Splash* and *Gung Ho*, wrote the screenplay along with Howard. Brian Grazer, Howard's partner in Imagine Films, also had a hand in coming up with ideas for the movie. "We started by going around collecting anecdotes about family life," Howard explained.[12]

They talked about their own family experiences, and they had many to draw from. At that time, Howard's four children were all under the age of seven. Ganz, Mandel, and Grazer had a total of eleven children among them.

Parenthood, like *Cocoon*, was an ensemble movie. That meant that there was a large cast and several different story lines. It was a style Howard liked. *American Graffiti* was also that type of movie, and the television shows he worked on had many characters. Each cast member got a chance to star at some time.

The cast for *Parenthood* includes Jason Robards, Steve Martin, Dianne Wiest, Mary Steenburgen, Keanu Reeves, Martha Plimpton, and Rick Moranis. "We had a lot of personalities here and these are people who are all used to being leads in movies," Howard said. "So that was something that I was dreading in a way." [13] There was a chance that cast members might complain that their parts were too small. It did not happen. Howard said everyone worked as a team and seemed to enjoy doing the movie.

Cast members were also encouraged to contribute their ideas. Howard said that the original script had very few lines for a scene where Steve Martin's character throws a birthday party for his son. Instead, the cast came up with ideas from their own experiences.

Steve Martin does a trick where he makes it appear that he has lost his thumb, scaring a little girl at the party. Rick Moranis thought of having a grandma sucking helium out of a balloon. Howard remembered a time when he was a child and had trouble trying to break a piñata. He finally ended up using a baseball bat on it. That also became part of the birthday party segment.

Howard had special problems to handle in directing *Parenthood*. One of them was that not all the cast members were available for the entire time that it took to film the movie. Howard juggled the shooting schedule, making sure that scenes were filmed on days when the stars could be on the set. "I felt like an air-traffic controller instead of a director sometimes," he said. [14]

The cast also includes many child actors and actresses, which created confusion on the set. Howard believes the key to directing child stars is to treat them as individuals—finding what works with each child. One three-year-old actor in the movie got fussy after a few takes of a scene. When that happened, Howard goofed around with the child, holding him upside down to get his mind on having fun.

In spite of the confusion on the set, Howard sometimes found it was the calmest place he could be. "There were some days where I was leaving my kids, who were having a bad day, and going to the set was peaceful compared to home," he said.[15]

"Home" in this case, was in Orlando, Florida, where *Parenthood* was being filmed. His work made it hard for Howard to find time to spend with his family, so he took them with him whenever he could. His children were often on the set, and he directed some scenes for *Parenthood* while he held one of his own children on his lap.

Howard also had other family members on the set. In one part of the movie, Steve Martin's character is a coach for his son's Little League team. Clint Howard appears in that scene as an obnoxious parent in the stands. Howard likes casting his brother in bad-guy roles, and it has become a family joke. Howard's father, Rance, also has a bit part in the film as a college president.

Parenthood was the type of movie that people expected from Howard—a lighthearted comedy. It was number one at the box office in its first two weeks of release, and it grossed more than $100 million. Ralph

Novak summed up the public's response to the movie in a review for *People* magazine: "Here is one great American movie."[16]

That year, 1989, Howard got a reminder of how important his family was to him. His mother had heart problems and had to have bypass surgery. Howard said it was a painful time, but he was also moved by the courage his mother showed during her illness.[17]

In the meantime, Howard was preparing for his next movie. Henry Fonda had given Howard some career advice when they worked together on the television series *The Smith Family*. "Every eighteen months you've got to risk your career and frighten yourself, or else you're not growing," Fonda said.[18]

Howard tries to follow that advice. Although reviewers of *Willow* said he could not handle action scenes, Howard was ready to try again with his next film, a story about a family of Irish-American firefighters.

Living and Learning

The title for Howard's next film, *Backdraft*, is the word used to describe an explosion that can occur during a fire. It happens when a fire burns up all the oxygen in a room. What is left are other gases, which explode if even a small amount of oxygen is let into the room. It means that if a fireman breaks a window or opens a door, there is a chance for a backdraft, or explosion.

Once again Howard was working on a movie that required special effects, but in a different way. Using special effects to film *Cocoon*, a movie about space aliens, was not the same as creating the fiery scenes of *Backdraft*. "It's more difficult to shoot fire scenes than fantasy," Howard said, "because no one really knows what an alien spacecraft is supposed to look like."[1]

As always, Howard paid careful attention to details. Before filming began, he had the actors spend three weeks training with real firefighters. The film was shot on location in Chicago, and firefighters were hired as technical advisors on the set. Howard also used Chicago firefighters for small roles in the movie. When he needed someone to ad-lib a line, the firefighters knew just what to say.

The people of Chicago appeared eager to work with Howard on the movie. One example was when he wanted to film a funeral scene on Michigan Avenue. It was a huge request. The busy, downtown street would have to be closed to traffic for five to six hours for filming on the day of a Chicago Bears game. Football fans had to detour around the area where they were filming, but Howard got his wish.

Howard also asked for a few hundred firefighters to be in the funeral scene. On the day of filming, about six hundred firefighters came. They were wearing their dress blue uniforms, just as they would have for the funeral of one of their own. They were volunteer extras in the film, but by being in the scene, they were eligible to win a car that was used in the film.

Backdraft got mixed reactions from critics when it was released in 1991. Most reviewers liked the special effects, but they thought the story was weak. A reviewer for *Variety* wrote: "The spectacular fire scenes are done with terrifying believability (usually with the actors in the same shot as the fire effects) and a kind of sci-fi grandeur."[2] On the other hand, a

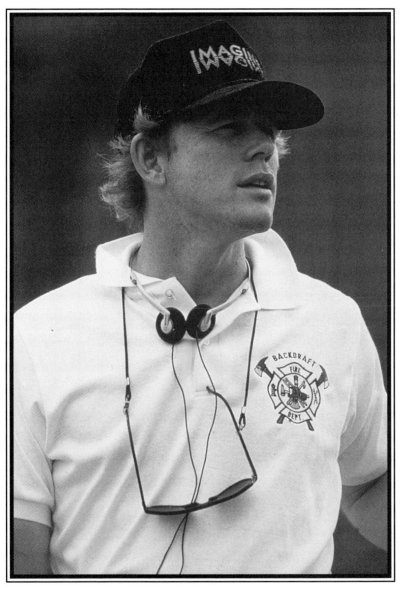

Howard on the set of the movie Backdraft. *Some people think he wears baseball caps to cover his thinning hair. Howard says that he was wearing the ever-present caps even before he began losing his hair.*

critic for *People* called the movie a "giant cornball of an action film."[3]

Still, audiences loved it. *Backdraft* became one of the highest-grossing movies of 1991. It also got the attention of the Academy Awards committee and won three awards—Best Sound, Best Sound Effects Editing, and Best Visual Effects.

Fans got a chance to experience the special effects up close when Universal Studios built a theme park ride based on the movie. Howard had a hand in creating it. He also made a test run and noted that the ride scared even him. "You can feel the heat on that ride," he said.[4]

In the spring of 1992, Howard returned to television for a *Happy Days* reunion. Henry Winkler hosted the special, which aired on March 3. The show featured clips from the series and interviews with the cast. In May, Howard's next film, *Far and Away*, was released.

Tom Cruise and Nicole Kidman star in that movie as two Irish immigrants who hear about free land that is being given away in Oklahoma. They arrive in Boston and work their way west to take part in one of the Oklahoma land rushes.

The Oklahoma land runs are a part of American history. There were a total of five, with the first taking place in April 1889. That was when the United States government bought two million acres of land from American Indians and made it available to white settlers. There was not enough land for everyone, so the settlers competed in a race to make their claims.

People began arriving days before the race began

and camped near the starting line. Soldiers were on hand to keep people from crossing the line to make their claim before the race began. They were not always successful. Some people got past the soldiers and found land they wanted to claim. They hid there until the day of the race. Then they rode their horses around in circles to make them look as tired as if they had been in the race.

More races were held as the government bought more land from American Indians and made it available to white settlers. The largest race took place on September 16, 1893. That was the race portrayed in the movie *Far and Away*.

Thousands of people gathered at the starting line that day. At noon, a gunshot signaled the beginning of the race and the rush began. People rode on horseback or in wagons loaded with all their belongings. Some were on foot and others pedaled bicycles. It was a dangerous race, with wagons overturning and riders being thrown from their horses. Once they got to their claims, violence broke out as settlers fought over the same pieces of land.

That bit of American history was also part of Howard's family history. "I had two great-grandfathers and one grandfather who rode in the original race," Howard noted.[5] In the movie, the Cruise and Kidman characters are successful in getting land, but Howard said his family was not so lucky. Only about one in a hundred people were able to stake their claims in the actual race. Howard's ancestors were not among the fortunate.

In the movie, Clint Howard plays a foreman in a

Boston factory sweatshop where Kidman's character works. Rance Howard also has a part in the film. He made a point of never interfering with his son's directing, but this time he had a special request. He wanted to ride in the race scene.

Crew members told Howard that it would be too risky for his dad to ride. They wanted to use stunt people. That made sense to Howard, who informed his dad that he would not be in the scene.

Rance Howard made one last plea. Later, in a television interview, Ron Howard told a reporter what his father had said: "Look, my great-grandfather rode in this race ninety-nine years ago, and now my son is making a movie about it, and I'd really appreciate it if you'd let me be in the shot."[6]

"He got his way," Ron Howard noted.[7]

Much of the movie was filmed in Montana, but part of it was also shot on location in Ireland. Howard said he enjoyed making the film. He liked working with Cruise and Kidman and they went to great locations. "The experience was perfect up until the film's release," Howard said.[8]

Howard was concerned about how successful the film would be commercially because it had a historical setting. It is what is known as a "period film." On the other hand, he was certainly not prepared for the blasting he received from film critics. They found fault with not only the movie but also Howard's abilities as a director. An example was a review for *Entertainment Weekly* in which a critic called Howard "an over-controlled Steven Spielberg wannabe."[9]

Howard says he does not read reviews when his

movies are first released. However, he does eventually read them. "Later, I get them as a stack and look at them and I often learn something about the film," he explained.[10]

Poor reviews for *Far and Away* kept people out of the theaters. The movie, which reportedly cost $60 million to produce, made only $29 million at the box office. With worldwide distribution, it eventually earned enough money to break even. Although the studio did not actually lose money on the film, the lack of interest in it was a big disappointment for Howard.[11]

At the same time, he was being criticized for another reason. The six-year contract that Howard and Grazer had signed with the stockholders of Imagine Films would expire in November 1992. Just before the release of *Far and Away*, Howard and Grazer announced that they would not renew that contract.

Part of their decision was based on money. For their work, they were paid fees that were about the same as other directors and producers made. The difference was that about half of their earnings were then reinvested in the company. As a result, they were making much less than they were worth.

Another reason for their decision was that they were being forced to become corporate businessmen. The company had been very successful in making movies. It had produced four $100-million movies, including Howard's *Parenthood* and *Backdraft*. The other two (not directed by Howard) were *Kindergarten Cop* (1990) starring Arnold Schwarzenegger and *My*

Girl (1991) with Macaulay Culkin and Anna Chlumsky.

Unfortunately, the movie business was not enough. If stockholders were going to profit from their investment, Howard and Grazer had to branch out into other areas such as buying television stations. They wanted to stick with what they did best—making movies.

Between them, Howard and Grazer already owned 54 percent of the company's stock. Universal Studios, which distributed most of their films, owned another 24 percent. Howard and Grazer proposed to buy the rest of the stock at $9 a share.

Stockholders were angry that Howard and Grazer were putting such a low value on their holdings. The original stockholders had paid $8 a share, but later the price was sometimes higher, making their shares worth much more.

One stockholder said that he had used his life savings to buy thirty thousand shares at about $10 a share. "The reason was, I had complete faith in Ron Howard as an honest person," he said.[12] Now that stockholder was about to lose money on his investment, and he blamed Howard. Investors said that Howard was getting greedy.

Some investment analysts said that $12 to $13 a share would be a fairer price for the stock. On the other hand, analysts noted that what was happening at Imagine was part of a trend. The same thing was happening at other film companies. The analysts said that entertainment companies were a risky investment and that stockholders should have known that.

Howard with Brian Grazer, his Imagine Films Entertainment partner. Howard and Grazer made stockholders angry when they decided to go private with their company.

The stockholders were not forced to sell to Howard and Grazer. The two partners had said that if they could not buy the stock, they would leave the company when their contract was up. The company could continue as Imagine Films Entertainment with new owners. However, stockholders believed that the company would not be successful without Howard and Grazer.

It would be several months before a final decision about the company was made. In the meantime, Howard decided to take a break. For the first time in several years, he did not spend the summer filming a new movie. Instead, he read, relaxed, and watched old films. He had kept journals during the filming of all his movies and that summer he read them again. After the harsh criticism he had received on *Far and Away*, it seemed that he needed time to think about what he wanted to do next.

While he was pondering his future, Steven Spielberg suggested that Howard meet with screen-writer David Koepp. Spielberg was impressed with Koepp because of the job he had done in co-writing a script for one of Spielberg's movies, *Jurassic Park*. Koepp was now working on another script, and Spielberg thought the topic would interest Howard.

Howard and Koepp got together, but all Koepp wanted to talk about was Howard's movie *Parenthood*. Koepp told Howard that he was using *Parenthood* as his guide in writing his own script, which, like *Parenthood*, had several story lines. "I found that pretty flattering, of course, so I asked about the subject of his work-in-progress," Howard recalled.

"The answer was music to my ears: twenty-four hours at a tabloid newspaper."[13]

The word tabloid is used to describe the newspapers that print attention-grabbing stories, such as articles about aliens from outer space or gossip about celebrities. However, tabloid also refers to a type of newspaper with pages about one half the size of a regular newspaper's. The smaller size makes it easier for commuters to read them on subways and trains on their way to work.

Koepp's brother Stephen was working with him on the script. Stephen Koepp had once been a newspaper reporter in Milwaukee. He was now a senior editor at *Time* magazine.

In April 1993, Howard, Grazer, and Imagine Films Entertainment announced that their deal was closed. According to reports, Universal Studios lent Howard and Grazer $24 million to buy the remaining company shares. They began operating as a private company under the name Imagine Entertainment.

By that time, Howard was doing research for his new movie, *The Paper*. As always, he was interested in accuracy. He spent about a month hanging out in the newsrooms of two New York newspapers. He sat in on editorial meetings and spent time talking to reporters and asking them questions. It was great fun for him because of his longtime interest in journalism.

The film features an all-star cast, including Michael Keaton, Marisa Tomei, Glenn Close, Robert Duvall, Randy Quaid, Jason Robards, and Jason Alexander. Keaton starred in two other Howard movies—*Night Shift* and *Gung Ho*. In *The Paper* he plays Henry Hackett, the news editor of a fictional tabloid newspaper called *The Sun*.

In the movie, Hackett struggles to balance a demanding career with his personal life—a problem that Howard experienced in his own life. "When my wife and I have arguments and conflicts, nine out of ten times it boils down to, 'How are you managing your time? Did you really need to do that?'" Howard explained.[14]

Two years earlier, when Howard was filming *Backdraft*, he had cast real firefighters in small roles. He used that technique again in *The Paper*, hiring journalists to play themselves in the movie. Clint and Rance Howard also have parts in the film, and Howard's wife, Cheryl, has a small role. She plays a character listed in the film credits as "red-headed barmaid."

Howard brought the movie in about $1.5 million under budget. He kept the cost down by filming in only one location and by completing the movie in fewer days than expected. The entire movie was shot in Manhattan, and Howard finished filming eight days ahead of schedule, even though a fire in the area interrupted shooting for a short time.

The firefighters could not help but note the irony of having a Ron Howard movie production interrupted by fire. One of them walked up to Howard and joked, "We'll be out of here in a few minutes. This ain't no *Backdraft*, Ron."[15]

The movie got good reviews, but it never caught on in the theaters. Box office receipts were even less than *Far and Away* had earned. Fortunately, *The Paper* had cost less to make. Howard could not explain why the movie did not do better. "You just live and learn," he said, "and in my case I've learned that I don't know."[16]

In the meantime, Brian Grazer heard about a book titled *Lost Moon: The Perilous Voyage of Apollo 13*. Jim Lovell, the commander of that space mission, was the author of the book. Many people were interested in getting the rights to make a movie about it. It was what is known in Hollywood as a hot property.

10

Ron Howard Is "A.O.K."

Howard did not remember much about the actual *Apollo 13* flight. He was sixteen years old at the time and was on location filming a guest appearance for the television series *Gunsmoke*. "We were staying out in the desert and the hotel didn't have a TV," he recalled. "And all I remember was that people were holding transistor radios to their ears, trying to keep up with the flight."[1]

Howard decided he was interested in directing the movie based on that flight after talking to astronaut Jim Lovell. "It was a riveting hour and a half," Howard said about their conversation. "It was one of those true stories that laid out like a movie."[2]

Tom Hanks was hired to play Lovell in the film.

Howard said he had wanted to work with him again ever since Hanks had starred in *Splash*. They had just never been able to get together on another project.

Hanks was happy to have the chance to play Lovell in the movie. He was a longtime space fan. As a child, he used kits to build models of the various spacecraft. He watched television coverage of all the space flights, and he knew the astronauts' names and which missions they flew.

Bill Paxton and Kevin Bacon star in the roles of Fred Haise and Jack Swigert, the other two astronauts on the *Apollo 13* mission. Gary Sinise plays astronaut Thomas Mattingly, who had been assigned to the flight but was bumped at the last minute after being exposed to measles. NASA did not want to take the chance that he might become sick with measles during the mission. Jack Swigert filled in for him on the flight, but Mattingly played a key role in finding a way to bring the astronauts home safely.

Before filming began, the actors spent hours at Mission Control in Houston, Texas, talking to real astronauts about what they did and how. They got firsthand experience in weightlessness aboard NASA's KC-135 jet. They also traveled to Huntsville, Alabama, where they flew a NASA simulator of the *Apollo* spacecraft.

A simulator is a vehicle that is like the actual spacecraft, but it never leaves the ground. Computers are used to make it appear that the spacecraft is in flight. Things that could go wrong during a mission are programmed into the computer. The simulator helps astronauts learn how to handle emergencies that may come up during a mission. It helped the

Apollo 13 actors learn how to look as if they were flying the spacecraft.

After the actors were trained for their roles as astronauts, filming began. It took four weeks just to shoot the weightlessness scenes aboard the KC-135 in Houston. The noise from the jet's engines was so loud that all of the actors' lines had to be re-recorded later in a studio.

Other scenes were filmed at Universal Studios in Los Angeles, California. The actors spent fourteen-hour days crammed inside the six-and-a-half-foot area that served as the lunar module. The *Apollo 13* astronauts had faced freezing temperatures in space. During the last five weeks of shooting, the temperature in the studio was kept at a bone-chilling thirty-four degrees Fahrenheit.

In spite of the realistic setting, Howard was sometimes reminded that he was working with actors pretending to be astronauts. He used a camera crane that lifted him above the lunar module so that he could look down inside it. "I'd be up on the camera crane and I'd look down, and there were Tom, Bill and Kevin, looking like any photo from the Apollo era. Yet they were discussing their agents, talking about how they used to wait tables—it was strange," he said.[3]

Howard also cast family members in the movie. His brother, Clint, plays a Mission Control technician, and his father has a small part as a minister. Howard's mother, Jean, plays the role of Lovell's mother, who was in a nursing home at the time of the flight.

Neil Armstrong and Buzz Aldrin, the two astronauts who made the first lunar landing, also have small roles in the movie. They appear as neighbors who try to distract Lovell's mother from the problems on *Apollo 13*.

When filming was done, Howard said he was proud of the movie, but he wondered if audiences would like it. "I have no idea if *Apollo 13* is going to be a hit," he said. "But I have to admit that this was the most awe-inspiring project I've ever worked on."[4]

It was a story Americans flocked to see, and critics liked it too. One reviewer called it "a powerhouse of a movie."[5] Another critic noted that even though everyone knew the outcome of the story, the movie was "tremendously suspenseful."[6] In a review for *America*, Richard A. Blake wrote: "*Apollo 13* is a wonderful

Howard with producer Brian Grazer on the set of Apollo 13.

summer movie. Kids will love the action, adults the character development and we codgers the memories. Come in Ron Howard. This is Movie Control. All systems are go. You're A.O.K."[7]

While Howard was working on *Apollo 13*, he heard about a story that was different from anything he had worked on so far. Even though Howard had directed a variety of movies, including comedy, drama, and fantasy, all his movies had one thing in common. They were what he calls celebrations—stories about people who overcome obstacles in their lives. "*Splash* celebrates love; *Parenthood*, the experience of child rearing; *Cocoon*, the idea that human beings have a reason to remain optimistic because extraordinary things can happen just around the corner," Howard explained.[8]

His next movie, a psychological thriller called *Ransom*, was about survival. Howard said he was interested in directing the film because he liked the characters. He also liked the story because it had a lot of twists and turns.

Ransom was a remake of a 1956 movie by the same name. Howard did not find out about the 1956 movie until about five weeks before they began filming his version. He was disappointed with that news because he had once promised himself he would never do a remake.[9] However, he noted that the 1996 movie was very different from the earlier one.

The movie stars Mel Gibson in the role of Tom Mullen, a wealthy airline executive whose son is kidnapped and held for ransom. When Mullen's attempt to pay the ransom goes bad, he makes an unusual decision. He says he will not pay the $2 million ransom. Instead, he offers $2 million as a reward for the capture of his son's kidnappers.

Rene Russo plays Mullen's wife, Kate. Gibson and Russo worked together previously in the 1992 movie *Lethal Weapon 3*.

Howard and Russo also knew each other before they got together for *Ransom*. They were classmates at Burroughs High School in Burbank, California. Howard said he never imagined that he would one day direct the shy girl he knew in high school. "If you'd said to me, 'Name ten students who might wind up acting,' Rene would have never made the list," Howard recalled.[10]

Nine-year-old Brawley Nolte plays the son who is held for ransom. He is the real-life son of actor Nick Nolte.

Filming was set to begin in New York City in mid-March 1996. Gibson, who lived in Los Angeles, flew to New York. During the flight, he began having abdominal pains. When the plane landed, he was rushed to a New York hospital. His appendix was infected and doctors had to remove it before it ruptured.

Howard began filming the movie without Gibson. "We just kept shooting and working around Mel," Howard told a reporter from the *Los Angeles Times*.[11] Later, they went back and plugged him into the scenes.

There were more delays in filming when New York was hit with some of the worst blizzards in that area in six years. The movie was supposed to take place in the winter. The delays meant that parts of the movie were being shot in April, when buds were beginning to appear on the trees. "Logistically, I can't say I've ever had worse on a movie," Howard said. "It was a real reworking of the whole schedule—it was a jigsaw puzzle."[12]

In spite of scheduling problems, Howard did not lose his sense of humor. After working in a small spacecraft on *Apollo 13*, he was enjoying the luxury of filming in a larger area. "I feel like I'm shooting in the Grand Canyon," he joked. "This time, I've got more than a six-and-a-half-foot capsule to work in."[13]

The movie had been scheduled for a late-summer release. Because of the delays in filming, it was moved to November. During the first weekend of its release, it pulled in more than $35 million at the box office.

In a review for *The New York Times*, Janet Maslin called the film "a spellbinding crime tale that delivers surprises right down to the wire."[14] In *People*, Leah Rozen wrote: "A slick, slam-bang thriller . . . *Ransom* is meant to divert and entertain. It does."[15]

There was negative criticism about the movie too. Critics said there were too many scenes showing the kidnapped son lying on a cot with his eyes covered with duct tape. Howard said it was important to show the danger to the child because that was the source of tension in the movie. He also reminded his critics that he was a father too. "As a parent, I sort of shot what I thought I could stand," he said.[16]

Celebrities such as actor/comedian Tim Allen felt shaken after seeing the movie. As soon as he left the theater, Allen called home to make sure his children were safe.

Howard was happy about that. "People wouldn't

take showers after they saw *Psycho*. They wouldn't go in the ocean after they saw *Jaws*. We hoped to make a suspenseful and thrilling movie and it's nice to know the audience is getting emotionally involved," he said.[17]

Some people said the movie was a sign that Howard might be starting to take more risks as a director. Howard's partner, Brian Grazer, said that the movie gave Howard a chance to express a side of himself that people usually did not see. "Ron seems to be a cheerful, easy-going guy," Grazer said. "But inside is a very complex, very competitive person who has darkness and pain. . . . And this movie was a creative way for him to express that."[18]

In 1997, Milan Records released *Passions & Achievements: A 20-Year Retrospective of Soundtracks from Films of Director Ron Howard*. The project is a

Howard directs a scene from Ransom *with actor Mel Gibson.*

salute to Howard's twentieth anniversary as a major motion picture director. It includes music from all twelve of the movies Howard directed in his first twenty years.

Twenty years as a director was an amazing achievement for Howard, who was then only forty-three years old. Even more incredible is his rise from the child star of a television series to motion-picture director. Howard knows it is something few people have been able to do. He says that sometimes when he is watching television, he asks himself, "Which of these people would I pick to be a high-profile movie director fifteen years from now?"[19] It is impossible to come up with an answer.

Howard has spent almost his entire life in the entertainment business. The pressures of that business have ruined the lives of some, but Howard seems unaffected. He is normal, likable, and, most of all, happy doing what he does. "I feel like that kid who grew up in the shadow of Yankee Stadium and suddenly finds himself playing centerfield in the World Series there," he said.[20]

He does not think he has reached his peak yet as a director. "I've always believed that I'd do my best work from age fifty to sixty-five," he once said.[21] That means there is much more to come from director Ron Howard.

1954—Born on March 1 in Duncan, Oklahoma.

1959—Makes his film debut in *The Journey*.

1960 —Stars as Opie Taylor in the television series *The*
-1968   *Andy Griffith Show*; also appears in big-screen movies, including *The Music Man* (1962), *The Courtship of Eddie's Father* (1963), and *Village of the Giants* (1965).

1971—Premiere of the television series *The Smith Family*; Ronny and his brother, Clint, star in the movie *The Wild Country*.

1972—Last episode of *The Smith Family* is shown; graduates from Burroughs Senior High School in Burbank, California; enrolls in the cinema studies program at the University of Southern California.

1973—Stars in the film *American Graffiti*.

1974—Premiere of the television series *Happy Days*, in which he stars in the role of Richie Cunningham.

1975—Marries Cheryl Alley on June 7.

1976—Stars in the Roger Corman film *Eat My Dust*; also appears in *The Shootist* with John Wayne.

1977—Director, co-writer, and star of the movie *Grand Theft Auto*.

1978—Directs his first made-for-television movie, *Cotton Candy*.

1979—Appears in the movie *More American Graffiti*, a sequel to *American Graffiti*.

1980—Leaves *Happy Days* to pursue a career as a director; directs *Skyward*, a made-for-television movie.

1981—Stars in the television movies *Bitter Harvest* and *Fire on the Mountain*; directs a two-part television movie, *Through the Magic Pyramid*; daughter Bryce is born.

1982—*Night Shift* is released.

1984—Premiere of *Splash*.

1985—Twin daughters, Jocelyn and Paige, are born; *Cocoon* is released.

1986—*Gung Ho* is released; appears as Opie Taylor in the television movie *Return to Mayberry*; moves his family to Connecticut; he and partner Brian Grazer found Imagine Films Entertainment, a public company.

1987—Son, Reed, is born.

1988—Release of *Willow*.

1989—Co-writer and director of the movie *Parenthood*.

1991—*Backdraft* is released.

1992—*Far and Away* premieres.

1993—Howard and Brian Grazer take their company private.

1994—*The Paper* is released.

1995—Release of *Apollo 13*.

1996—Receives the Outstanding Directorial Achievement in Motion Picture award from the Directors Guild of America for his work on *Apollo 13*; premiere of *Ransom*.

1997—Milan Records releases *Passions & Achievements: A 20-Year Retrospective of Soundtracks from Films of Director Ron Howard* as a salute to Howard's first twenty years as a director.

Ron Howard Performs

The Andy Griffith Show, 1960–1968, television series
The Music Man, 1962
American Graffiti, 1973
Happy Days, 1974–1980, television series
The Shootist, 1976
Grand Theft Auto, 1977 (also director and screenwriter)

Ron Howard Directs

Night Shift, 1982
Splash, 1984
Cocoon, 1985
Gung Ho, 1986 (also producer)
Willow, 1988
Parenthood, 1989
Backdraft, 1991
Far and Away, 1992 (also producer)
The Paper, 1994
Apollo 13, 1995
Ransom, 1996

Chapter Notes

Chapter 1. Filming in the Vomit Comet

1. Kim Cunningham, "A Ron by Any Other Name," *People*, November 22, 1993, p. 130.

2. Kim Cunningham, "Those Uppity Actors," *People*, March 25, 1996, p. 122.

3. Richard Corliss, "Hell of a Ride," *Time*, July 3, 1995, p. 52.

4. James Rosenfield, "Ron Howard: Director of *Apollo 13*," *Media Magazine*, July 1995. On the Internet at <http://www.gigaplex.com/film/apollo/howard.htm>

5. Eleanor Mondale, *Uncut*, live broadcast on E!, November 3, 1996.

6. Ibid.

7. Rosenfield.

8. Corliss, p. 53.

9. Owen Gleiberman, "Apollo 13" (movie review), *Entertainment Weekly*, June 30, 1995, p. 78.

10. Ralph Novak, "Apollo 13" (movie review), *People,* July 3, 1995, p. 19.

Chapter 2. Opie

1. Edwin Miller, "Straight, No Square!" *Seventeen*, March 1975, p. 100.

2. Marian Dern, "Ronny and Clint Howard—Two Brothers, Two Shows," *TV Guide*, March 13–19, 1965, p. 26.

3. Miller, p. 100.

4. Ibid.

5. Patrick Goldstein, "Ron Howard Making a Big 'Splash,'" *Los Angeles Times*, March 26, 1984, part 6, p. 2.

6. Warren Kalbacker, "Ron Howard," *Playboy*, May 1994, p. 56.

7. Dennis Washburn, "Ron Howard: He's Still Growing and Learning," *Birmingham News* (Birmingham, Ala.), November 22, 1981, p. 48.

8. Desmond Ryan, "'Cocoon' Unfolds, a Talent Takes Wing," *Philadelphia Inquirer*, June 29, 1985.

9. Susan Sackett, *The Hollywood Reporter Book of Box Office Hits* (New York: Billboard Books, 1990), p. 165.

10. Betty Goodwin, "In Mayberry, You *Can* Go Home Again," *TV Guide*, April 12, 1986, p. 48.

11. Stephen J. Spignesi, *Mayberry My Hometown: The Ultimate Guidebook to America's Favorite TV Small Town* (Ann Arbor: Popular Culture, Ink., 1991), p. 227.

12. Jane Hall, "Going Home to Mayberry," *People*, April 14, 1986, p. 97.

13. Richard Kelly, *The Andy Griffith Show* (Winston-Salem: John F. Blair, 1981), p. 129.

14. Joseph Gelmis, "A Fountain of Youth," *Newsday* (Long Island, N.Y.), June 23, 1985.

15. David Brooks, "'Gung Ho' Howard," *Washington Times* (Washington, D.C.), March 14, 1986.

16. "On Top of the World: Ron Howard Keeps Going . . . and Going . . . " *Cedar Rapids Gazette*, November 28, 1996, p. 3C.

Chapter 3. *American Graffiti*

1. Dotson Rader, "A Nice Guy and a Winner," *Parade*, November 10, 1996, p. 5.

2. Patrick Goldstein, "Ron Howard Making a Big 'Splash,'" *Los Angeles Times*, March 26, 1984, part 6, p. 2.

3. Rader, p. 6.

4. Yardena Arar, "Ron 'Scoop' Howard: Director Finally Gets to Play Journalist Role," *Daily News* (Los Angeles), March 26, 1994.

5. Ellen Pfeifer, "Opie Grows Up," *Herald American* (Boston), July 30, 1982.

6. Warren Kalbacker, "Ron Howard," *Playboy*, May 1994, p. 61.

7. Joseph Kanon, "Movies: On the Strip," *Atlantic*, October 1973, p. 125.

8. Stephen Farber, "'Graffiti' Ranks With 'Bonnie and Clyde,'" *The New York Times*, August 5, 1973, sec. 2, p. 1.

Chapter 4. *Happy Days*

1. Edwin Miller, "Straight, No Square!" *Seventeen*, March 1975, p. 101.

2. Lawrence Laurent, "'Happy Days' Turns Back Clock to the 1950s," *Washington Post*, February 24, 1974, *TV Channels*, p. 5.

3. Ann Hodges, "Those Were 'Happy Days' for Young Cast," *Houston Chronicle*, March 3, 1992.

4. Vincent Canby, movie review, *The New York Times*, May 2, 1974, p. 61.

5. Lois Armstrong, "Happy Days Are Here Forever, as Ron Howard Plays Cecil B. in the Big D," *People*, June 12, 1978, p. 94.

6. Judy Klemesrud, "The Kid Wanted to Direct," *The New York Times*, June 22, 1977, p. C15.

7. Warren Kalbacker, "Ron Howard," *Playboy*, May 1994, p. 57.

8. Ibid.

9. Todd McCarthy, "Auteur Opie," *Film Comment*, May/June 1984, p. 41.

10. Dennis Washburn, "Ron Howard: He's Still Growing and Learning," *Birmingham News* (Birmingham, Ala.), November 22, 1981.

11. Mal Vincent, "Opie Finds Happy Days in Director's Chair," *Virginian-Pilot* (Norfolk, Va.), November 23, 1981.

Chapter 5. Getting a Start

1. Yardena Arar, "For Howard, Father of Four, Art Imitates Life," *Daily News* (Los Angeles), August 3, 1989.

2. Paul Rosenfield, "Happy Days' Ron Howard: Life Begins After High School," *Los Angeles Times*, August 19, 1977, part 4, p. 13.

3. Judy Klemesrud, "The Kid Wanted to Direct," *The New York Times*, June 22, 1977, p. C15.

4. Lawrence Van Gelder, "Demolition Derby," *The New York Times*, September 29, 1977, p. C19.

5. Klemesrud, p. C15.

6. Lois Armstrong, "Happy Days Are Here Forever, as Ron Howard Plays Cecil B. in the Big D," *People*, June 12, 1978, p. 92.

7. Ibid.

8. Ibid.

9. David Ansen, "Sliding Downhill in the '60s," *Newsweek*, August 27, 1979, p. 63.

10. Louis B. Parks, "The Man Behind 'The Paper': Ron Howard's Leap From Acting to Directing in '80 Was a Risk That Paid Off," *Houston Chronicle*, April 5, 1994.

11. Samir Hachem, "The Metamorphosis of Ron Howard," *Horizon*, June 1985, p. 23.

12. Ibid.

13. Todd McCarthy, "Auteur Opie," *Film Comment*, May/June 1984, p. 41.

Chapter 6. "Opie Cunningham"

1. Judith Crist, "This Week's Movies," *TV Guide*, May 16–22, 1981, p. A-6.

2. Tom Green, "Happy Days Spent Behind the Camera," *USA Today*, June 24, 1985, p. D2.

3. Todd McCarthy, "Auteur Opie," *Film Comment*, May/June, 1984, p. 41.

4. Warren Kalbacker, "Ron Howard," *Playboy*, May 1994, p. 56.

5. Ibid., p. 54.

6. Stephen Farber, "Ron Howard: From Hot Act to Hot Director," *The New York Times Biographical Service*, June 1985, p. 711.

7. Jim Jerome, "A Whale of a Tail," *People*, April 9, 1984, p. 36.

8. Ibid., p. 37.

9. Joe Pollack, "Ron Howard: Changing Direction," *St. Louis Post-Dispatch*, June 20, 1985.

10. Jerome, p. 38.

11. Richard Schickel, "Of Hotels, Hoods and a Mermaid," *Time*, March 19, 1984, p. 91.

12. Pauline Kael, "King Candy," *New York*, March 19, 1984, p. 123.

13. Dick Kleiner, "Howard Leads an Older Cast," *Express News* (San Antonio, Tex.), January 4, 1985.

14. David Ansen, "Like a Fish Out of Water," *Newsweek*, March 12, 1984, p. 89.

15. Douglas D. Armstrong, "He's Still Opie," *Milwaukee Journal*, June 23, 1985.

Chapter 7. "From Tyke to Tycoon"

1. Joseph Gelmis, "A Fountain of Youth," *Newsday* (Long Island, N.Y.), June 23, 1985.

2. Ibid.

3. Samir Hachem, "The Metamorphosis of Ron Howard," *Horizon*, June 1985, p. 24.

4. Ibid.

5. Michael Healy, "Ron Howard Can't Shed 'Opie,'" *Denver Post*, June 9, 1985.

6. Warren Kalbacker, "Ron Howard," *Playboy*, May 1994, p. 58.

7. Stephen J. Spignesi, *Mayberry My Hometown: The Ultimate Guidebook to America's Favorite TV Small Town* (Ann Arbor: Popular Culture, Ink., 1991), p. 222.

8. Interview by Bryant Gumbel on *Today*. Live broadcast on NBC-TV, November 6, 1996.

9. David Brooks, "'Gung Ho' Howard," *Washington Times*, March 14, 1986.

10. "Teen Then & Now: Ron Howard," *Teen*, April 1986, p. 74.

11. Ralph Novak, "Picks & Pans," *People*, March 31, 1986, p. 8.

12. Jane Hall, "Going Home to Mayberry," *People*, April 14, 1986, p. 92.

13. Peter Gethers, "A Night of Vice with Mr. Nice," *Esquire*, December 1986, p. 258.

14. Ibid.

15. Hall, p. 97.

16. Sheryl Kahn, "Fathers Know Best: Mel Gibson and Ron Howard Trade Tales About Raising Normal Kids in Hollywood. (Is It Possible?)," *McCall's*, August 1996, p. 42.

17. Meredith Berkman, "Paper Boy," *Entertainment Weekly*, April 1, 1994.

18. Gethers, p. 258.

19. Ibid.

20. Jeffrey Ressner, "Nice Guy at Mission Control," *Time*, July 3, 1995, p. 53.

21. "Splash in the Stock Market," *Time*, August 4, 1986, p. 56.

Chapter 8. From Fantasy to Real Life

1. Malcolm L. Johnson, "Howard Fulfilling Fantasies With Extravagant 'Willow,'" *Hartford Courant* (Hartford, Conn.), May 20, 1988.

2. Howie Movshovitz, "Ron Howard and Parenthood," *Denver Post*, August 4, 1989.

3. Craig Tomashoff, "Ron Howard," *Middlesex News* (Framingham, Mass.), May 22, 1988.

4. Michael Janusonis, "Ron Howard: The Gee Whiz Kid," *Providence Journal* (Providence, R.I.), May 20, 1988.

5. Johnson.

6. Tomashoff.

7. Johnson.

8. Joseph Dalton, "From Howard's Imagine-ings: Director Teams With Mentor Lucas to Create *Willow*," *Herald Examiner* (Los Angeles), May 19, 1988.

9. Bruce Williamson, "Willow" (movie review), *Playboy*, August 1988, p. 14.

10. Richard Corliss, "Willow" (movie review), *Time*, May 23, 1988, p. 79.

11. Movshovitz.

12. Gary Arnold, "Family Man Ron Howard: Easing into 'Parenthood,'" *Washington Times* (Washington, D.C.), August 8, 1989.

13. David Kronke, "Howard Returns to Movies About Families, Not Just Special Effects," *Dallas Times Herald*, August 6, 1989.

14. Ron Givens with Charles Leerhsen, "The Nice Guy Rides Again," *Newsweek*, August 28, 1989, p. 57.

15. Arnold.

16. Ralph Novak, "Picks & Pans," *People*, August 14, 1989, p. 17.

17. Dotson Rader, "Nice Guy and a Winner," *Parade*, November 10, 1996, p. 6.

18. Stephen Farber, "Ron Howard: From Hot Act to Hot Director," *New York Times Biographical Service*, June 1985, p. 712.

Chapter 9. Living and Learning

1. William E. Schmidt, "Chicago Goes for the Burn in the Making of *Backdraft*," *The New York Times*, January 20, 1991, sec. 2, p. 23.

2. Derek Elley (ed.), *Variety Movie Guide*, Hamlyn: U.K., Butterworth-Heinemann, 1995, p. 52.

3. Ralph Novak, "Picks & Pans," *People*, June 3, 1991, p. 15.

4. Warren Kalbacker, "Ron Howard," *Playboy*, May 1994, p. 147.

5. "Family Spirit Inspires Ron Howard for *Far and Away*," *Star-Ledger* (Newark, N.J.), May 24, 1992.

6. Eleanor Mondale, *Uncut*, live broadcast on E!, November 3, 1996.

7. Ibid.

8. Kalbacker, p. 63.

9. Owen Gleiberman, "Far and Away" (movie review), *Entertainment Weekly*, May 22, 1992.

10. Interview by Bryant Gumbel on *Today*. Live broadcast on NBC-TV, November 6, 1996.

11. Kalbacker, p. 63.

12. Matt Rothman and Claudia Eller, "Tepid Stock Price Steams Imagine Investors," *Variety*, May 11, 1992, p. 5.

13. Gary Arnold, "Tabloid Press Gets the Ron Howard Touch in *The Paper*," *Washington Times* (Washington, D.C.), March 27, 1994.

14. Yardena Arar, "Ron 'Scoop' Howard: Director Finally Gets to Play Journalist Role," *Daily News* (Los Angeles), March 26, 1994.

15. Kalbacker, p. 53.

16. Jerry Rice, "Ron Howard: Paying for His Ransom," *Entertainment Today*. On the Internet at <http://www.entertainment-today.com/Nov08-14/howard.html>

Chapter 10. Ron Howard Is "A.O.K."

1. Skip Hollandsworth, "Shooting the Moon: The Inside Story of the Making of *Apollo 13* (New Feature Film Directed by Ron Howard)," *Texas Monthly*, July 1995, starts on p. 92.

2. Pam Lambert and Todd Gold, "Aces in Space," *People*, July 3, 1995, p. 72.

3. Ibid., p. 73.

4. Hollandsworth.

5. Guy Flatley, "Apollo 13" (movie review), *Cosmopolitan,* August 1995, p. 32.

6. Brian D. Johnson, "Apollo 13" (movie review), *Maclean's,* July 10, 1995, p. 50.

7. Richard A. Blake, "Apollo 13" (movie review), *America,* July 29, 1995, starts on p. 30.

8. Dotson Rader, "A Nice Guy and a Winner," *Parade,* November 10, 1996, p. 6.

9. Interview by Bryant Gumbel on *Today.* Live broadcast on NBC-TV, November 6, 1996.

10. "Pre-Fab Stars," *People,* April 28, 1997, p. 50.

11. Bronwen Hruska, "They Can't Buy a Break," *Los Angeles Times,* April 21, 1996.

12. Ibid.

13. Kristen O'Neill, "'Ransom' Demands for Gibson, Howard, and Sinise," *Premiere,* May 1996, p. 21.

14. Janet Maslin, "Vigilante Dad vs. Kidnappers," *The New York Times,* November 8, 1996, p. C1.

15. Leah Rozen, "Ransom" (movie review), *People,* November 18, 1996, p. 20.

16. Bernard Weinraub, "The Dark Underbelly of Ron Howard," *The New York Times,* November 12, 1996, p. C12.

17. "*Ransom* a Chiller," *Cedar Rapids Gazette,* November 7, 1996, p. 9B.

18. Weinraub, p. C12.

19. Jerry Rice, "Ron Howard: Paying for His Ransom," *Entertainment Today.* On the Internet at <http://www.entertainment-today.com/Nov08-14/howard.html>

20. "On Top of the World: Ron Howard Keeps Going . . . and Going . . ." *Cedar Rapids Gazette,* November 28, 1996, p. 3C.

21. Meredith Berkman, "Paper Boy," *Entertainment Weekly,* April 1, 1994, starts on p. 22.

Further Reading

Armstrong, Lois. "Happy Days Are Here Forever, as Ron Howard Plays Cecil B. in the Big D." *People*, June 12, 1978, pp. 90–96.

Jerome, Jim. "Whale of a Tail." *People*, April 9, 1984, pp. 34–39.

Kelly, Richard. *The Andy Griffith Show*. Winston-Salem, N.C.: John F. Blair, 1981.

Kluger, Jeffrey, and Ron Howard. *The Apollo Adventure: The Making of the Apollo Space Program and the Movie Apollo 13*. New York: Pocket Books, 1995.

Lambert, Pam and Todd Gold. *"Aces in Space." People*, July 3, 1995, pp. 70–73.

Spignesi, Stephen J. *Mayberry My Hometown: The Ultimate Guidebook to America's Favorite TV Small Town*. Ann Arbor: Popular Culture, Ink., 1991.

Books About Filmmaking

Platt, Richard. *Film*. New York: Knopf, 1992.

Scott, Elaine. *Movie Magic: Behind the Scenes with Special Effects*. New York: Morrow Junior Books, 1995.

On the Internet

"Biography from Baseline's Encyclopedia of Film."
<http://cinemania.msn.com/Person/Biography/1321>

Rice, Jerry. "Paying for His Ransom."
<http://www. entertainment-today.com/Nov08-14/howard.html>

Rosenfield, James. "Ron Howard: Director of Apollo 13."
<http://www.gigaplex.com/film/apollo/howard.htm>

Index